100 Ways
with Fish

Anne Ager

 Letts **Guides**

Charles Letts and Company Ltd
London Edinburgh München and New York

First published 1977
by Charles Letts and Company Limited
Diary House, Borough Road, London SE1 1DW

Design and illustrations by Ed Perera
Cover photograph by Andrew Thompson

© Anne Ager 1977
ISBN 0 850 97235 3

Printed in Great Britain by
Letts Erskine Limited, Dalkeith

Contents

Introduction

Fish has always been an important source of food for man. Until the beginning of the nineteenth century, however, it was only those people who lived near the sea or a large river who were able to eat fish regularly. There was at that time no method of large scale fishing, transportation or preservation.

With the introduction of trawling, railway transport and canning, fish became more widely available. Now, with new techniques in refrigeration and freezing and improvement in transport, it is possible for everyone to eat fish regularly.

Tastes and preferences vary as much for fish as for any other food, and this is not due only to availability. A fish scorned by the inhabitants of one country can be considered a great delicacy by the people of another. Many types of fish are unknown to us in this country: people of the Mediterranean countries, for example, consume a far greater variety of fish than the British do. We do not have the same abundance of fish from which to choose, and yet we are still a little reluctant to try some of the fish sold by British fishmongers. Neverthe-

less, once the different categories and methods of preparation are understood all fish are easy to cook.

There are six main categories of fish: white fish, oily fish, freshwater fish, smoked fish, shellfish and preserved fish (covering canned, jarred and frozen fish). One type is described in each of the following sections of this book, and recipes are given. The basic preparation and methods of cooking fish are described on pp 6-8 and recipes for sauces on pp 60-62.

Buying fish

Freshness is of the greatest importance. Fish is highly perishable, and it is advisable to buy it no more than a day before it is needed. Look for the following points:

- The eyes should be bright and protruding, not sunken.
- The gills should be brilliant red in colour.
- The scales should be compact and tightly attached to the skin.
- The flesh should feel firm to the touch, not limp.

A very reliable sign of freshness is the smell—the fish should retain the smell of the sea or river and be slightly slimy. The colour, too, is a good indicator. Filleted white fish and cutlets, for example plaice and cod, should be an opalescent white. Fillets with a dark underskin will appear less white and slightly discoloured. Any characteristic markings, such as the orange spots on plaice or the silvery sparkle of mackerel, should be clearly defined.

Special care must be taken when buying uncooked shellfish. Most shellfish is, in fact, sold ready cooked; dead, uncooked shellfish can cause food poisoning if it is not in perfect condition. These hints will help you to distinguish fresh shellfish from stale ones:

● The shells of mussels and oysters should be tightly shut; avoid any that have broken shells.
● Scallops should be pearly white and their curved roe brilliant orange.
● Lobster, crawfish, crabs and prawns should have tough shells and be brightly coloured.
● Any fish that has a trace smell of ammonia is stale.

Storing fish

Ideally fish should be bought on the day it is needed. This is not, however, always possible and if it is necessary to store the fish, be guided by these points:

● Remove fish from the fish-monger's wrapping.
● Do not wash it before storing as this will cause it to perish very quickly.

● Put it on to a clean plate and cover it loosely with foil or cling wrap. Tight wrapping will cause the fish to sweat, but it must be covered to prevent the smell spreading to other foods.
● Keep fish in the refrigerator until it is needed, but no more than one day.

To freeze fish, which is a long term method of storage:

for white, oily, smoked and fresh-water fish, prepare according to type—fish can be left whole, cut into cutlets or filleted (see p 6). Dip the fish into slightly salted cold water and drain well. Separate fillets or cutlets with pieces of waxed paper, wrap the fish in foil, freezer wrap or polythene bags and seal and label it. Frozen fish can be stored for up to six months, with the exception of smoked fish. Its storage time in the freezer is two months.

Shellfish such as lobster and crab must be bought live and killed just before freezing. Their storage time is very short, and most people would find freezing too complicated to be worthwhile.

For shrimps and prawns: boil in salted water for five to six minutes. Cool and drain. Remove the shells and pack the fish into waxed cartons. They can be stored for up to two months.

For oysters: remove from their shells, saving their juice. Rinse in salted water and drain. Pack into waxed cartons with their juice. They can be stored for up to two months.

Made up fish dishes, such as fish soups, casseroles and pies, should be wrapped and sealed, either in lidded foil dishes or in waxed cartons. Label them clearly and store for no more than two months.

Fish that is to be cooked slowly can be cooked from the frozen state, allowing a little extra time. Fish that is to be cooked fairly quickly should be thawed completely in its unopened wrapping. Allow it to thaw from four to six hours in a cool place.

Food value

Fish is as nourishing as best rump-steak and is very easy to digest. Its food value varies according to the type of fish, but all types have a high protein content and a good proportion of fat. The oily fish group, such as herring, is high in vitamins A and D, and in iron and calcium. White fish, such as cod, contain phosphorus, iodine, fluorine and iron. All white fish is particularly good for small children, invalids and those on a diet.

Preparation and methods of cooking

Most fishmongers prepare fish for you so that it is ready to cook, but it is worth knowing how to do it yourself. There are four main preparation stages: scaling, cleaning and gutting, skinning and filleting. Skinning and filleting apply only to the larger fish since small fish like herring are cooked in their skins.

To scale: scrape from the tail end of the fish to the head with the blunt edge of a knife, catching the scales on newspaper. Rinse the fish to remove any loose scales.

To clean and gut: if the head is not going to be cooked with the fish, remove it to make gutting easier. Then slit the belly of the fish open with a sharp knife and remove the entrails and any blood. Remove the fins. Rinse the fish quickly under cold running water, but do not wash it.

To skin: this is the procedure for skinning whole fish on the bone; only plaice are skinned after filleting. Lay the fish on a board and hold the tail firmly in one hand. Make a small incision near the tail to loosen the skin. Pull sharply to remove the skin in one piece. Repeat with the other side of the fish.

To fillet: the method varies according to the type of fish. For flat fish like plaice, put on a board and with a sharp knife make an incision from the tail to the head that penetrates the flesh but does not cut through the bone. Placing the blade of the knife in the cut that you have made, carefully ease the blade between the fillet and the bone—it should come away cleanly. Repeat with the other fillets.

For small round fish and herring, make a cut down the length of the fish, along its back. Insert the knife and ease the flesh from backbone.

There are eight basic methods of cooking fish: poaching, grilling, frying (shallow and deep), steaming, baking, braising, au gratin, and en papillotes (in an envelope).

Poaching is a gentle method of cooking fish in a flavoured liquid so that it will not disintegrate. The flavoured cooking liquid makes a good basis for a sauce. Whole fish, cutlets or fillets can be used. Put the fish into a shallow buttered pan with a little chopped onion. Add herbs, seasoning, and sufficient liquid, for example wine, cider or chicken stock, to come halfway up the depth of the fish. Cover the pan with a piece of buttered paper or foil and simmer the fish on top of the stove until it is just tender.

Grilling subjects the fish to direct heat and care should be taken not to allow the fish to become dry. Oily fish are ideal for grilling because of their natural fat content, but white fish can also be grilled. The grill should not be too high and regular basting is necessary to keep the fish moist. Brush the grill pan with fat and lay the seasoned fish on top. Brush the fish with extra fat and put it under the grill. Cook until the surface browns slightly or blisters. Turn the fish carefully and continue grilling until it is tender.

Frying: there are two different methods, deep frying, using a deep pan of hot fat and coated fish, and shallow frying, cooking the fish gently in a small amount of fat. For deep frying oil or lard are the fats generally used. Fish fillets or whole small fish can be deep fried, coated with egg and breadcrumbs, flour or batter (see p 61 for batter recipes). Heat sufficient fat to give a depth of about $2\frac{1}{2}$in. When there is a smoky haze over the fat it is hot enough. Lower the coated fish into the pan and cook it until golden and tender. Remove from the pan and drain.

Another name for shallow frying is *a la meuniere*. Oil, butter, or a mixture of both is generally used. Fillets or small whole fish can be shallow fried, just floured, or coated in crumbs. Heat sufficient fat in a shallow pan to cover the base evenly. Cook the fish gently on one side, turn and cook on the other.

Steaming is an ideal method of cooking fish for invalids or for small children as the cooked fish is very soft and easy to digest. A steamer can be used but it is just as easy to use a deep plate or shallow heatproof dish. Grease the plate generously with butter and lay the seasoned fish on top, either in fillets or small pieces. Top with extra butter and a little milk. Stand over a pan of boiling water and cover with a lid. Keep the water simmering gently until the fish is tender.

Baking is suitable for large and small whole fish and for cutlets; fillets are generally too thin. Fish can be baked without basting. Put the prepared seasoned fish into a greased ovenproof dish. Top with knobs of butter or a little sauce (see pp 60-62 for sauce recipes). Cover the dish with a piece of foil and bake in a moderate oven until the fish is tender.

Braising is a method of cooking large whole fish. It is best to use an oval casserole which will fit the shape of the fish. Place a bed of fried vegetables in the bottom (for example chopped celery, carrot and onion). Lay the prepared and seasoned fish on the top. Add enough liquid to just cover the vegetables. Cover with a lid and cook in a moderate oven until the fish is just tender.

Au gratin is really an adaptation of another method. The fish is usually first poached or baked and then 'finished' *au gratin*. The cooked fish is sprinkled with crumbs and dotted with butter and then browned under the grill or in the oven; or covered with a coating white sauce and sprinkled with grated cheese before browning.

En papillotes is a method of cooking fish in an envelope of foil or grease-proof paper to retain all the moisture, flavour and smell of the fish. Small whole fish, cutlets or fillets can be cooked in this way. Cut a piece of foil or greaseproof paper for each piece of fish, large enough to allow sufficient overlap to seal (foil is better as it is easier to seal). Grease the paper or foil and place the seasoned fish in the centre. Add a little butter and any extra flavouring desired, for example herbs, fried mushrooms or onion, or a little sauce (see pp 60-62). Fold the paper over the fish and pinch the edges to seal. Place the envelopes on a baking sheet and cook in a moderate oven until the fish is tender. It can be served in its packages.

Weights and measures

All ingredient quantities are given in British Standard measurements, and the appropriate American measures for each ingredient follow at the foot of every recipe. Note that American spoon measures are smaller than British spoons:

1 British teaspoon equals $1\frac{1}{4}$ American teaspoons

1 British tablespoon equals $1\frac{1}{4}$ American tablespoons.

The following metric equivalents apply for measuring ingredients, but note that metric measures are always given as convenient round figures and are only approximate equivalents. When converting large quantities one obtains slightly less of the finished product than when using ounces and pounds.

1 oz is taken as 25gm
4 oz are taken as 100gm
8 oz are taken as 200gm

1 lb is taken as 500gm
1 teaspoon is taken as 5ml
  (American teasp 4·8ml)
1 tablespoon is taken as 15ml
  (American tbsp 14·8ml)
$\frac{1}{4}$ pint is taken as 125ml
1 pint is taken as 500ml
2 pints are taken as 1 litre

Equivalent oven temperatures

250°F	Mark $\frac{1}{2}$	130°C
275°F	Mark 1	140°C
300°F	Mark 2	145°C
325°F	Mark 3	160°C
350°F	Mark 4	175°C
375°F	Mark 5	190°C
400°F	Mark 6	205°C
425°F	Mark 7	220°C
450°F	Mark 8	235°C

Abbreviations

teasp—teaspoon
tbsp—tablespoon
dessertsp—dessertspoon

All recipes that are marked with a star * are particularly suitable for freezing.

White fish

This group contains some of the most popular types of fish in this country. They are all sea bed dwellers, and the following twenty varieties are usually available throughout Great Britain: bass, brill, cod, coley, conger eel, dab, dogfish, flounder, gurnard, haddock, hake, halibut, plaice, redfish, sea bass, skate, sole, turbot, whiting. The names do, however, vary from one part of the country to another. Dogfish, for example, is known as rock salmon in many parts, and coley is often referred to as saithe.

White fish vary in appearance, size, texture and flavour, but most of them are suitable for all methods of cooking. Plaice, sole and whiting are sold both whole and in fillets, whereas most of the other white fish mentioned are either sold in fillets or cut into steaks. Most white fish is at its best during the winter months.

* Raised fish pie

Serves 4
$\frac{3}{4}$ lb cod fillet
$\frac{1}{2}$ lb smoked haddock
butter
1 small onion, chopped
$\frac{1}{4}$ pint white wine
$\frac{1}{4}$ pint milk
bay leaf
seasoning
$\frac{1}{4}$ lb button mushrooms, sliced
pinch grated nutmeg
3 hard-boiled eggs
grated rind $\frac{1}{2}$ lemon
1 lb shortcrust pastry
beaten egg
anchovy sauce (see p 60)

Put the fish into a buttered shallow pan with the onion, wine, milk, bay leaf and seasoning. Cover with a circle of buttered paper. Poach gently until fish is just tender— about 15 minutes, depending on thickness of fish. Drain fish, remove skin and discard any bones. Flake the fish. Cook mushrooms gently in a little butter with the grated nutmeg. Mix the fish with the mushrooms, coarsely chopped hard-boiled egg, grated lemon rind and seasoning. Moisten with a little poaching liquid. Roll out $\frac{2}{3}$ of the the pastry and use to line the base and sides of a $7\frac{1}{2}$–8in shallow loose-bottomed cake tin. Fill with the fish mixture. Roll out the remaining pastry. Brush pastry edges with beaten egg and cover with the pastry lid. Trim off excess pastry and pinch edges together to seal. Make a small air hole in the lid, and glaze with beaten egg—the top can be decorated with pastry leaves. Bake at 350°F, Mark 4, for $1\frac{1}{4}$ hours. Serve hot or cold with anchovy sauce.

(American: $1\frac{1}{4}$ cups flaked cod, $\frac{3}{4}$ cup flaked smoked haddock, $\frac{1}{2}$ cup milk, $\frac{1}{2}$ cup wine, $\frac{2}{3}$ cup mushrooms, 2 cups pastry)

* Samsoe fish flan

Serves 6
$\frac{1}{2}$ lb shortcrust pastry
1 onion
$1\frac{1}{2}$ oz butter
3 eggs
$\frac{1}{2}$ pint single cream
seasoning
6 oz cooked white fish
4 oz grated Samsoe cheese

Line an $8\frac{1}{2}$–9in flan dish with the pastry and prick the base. Fry the chopped onion gently in butter for 4 minutes. Beat the eggs with the cream and the seasoning and add the onion, flaked fish and 3 oz of the Samsoe. Pour into the pastry case. Sprinkle with remaining cheese. Bake at 375°F, Mark 5, for 45 minutes.

(American: 1 cup pastry, 3 tbsp butter, 1 cup single cream, $\frac{2}{3}$ cup cooked fish, $\frac{1}{2}$ cup Samsoe cheese)

Bouillabaisse

Serves 4

This is a typical Provencal fish stew. Almost any combination of fish can be used, but to make this tasty fish stew in Great Britain we can only use those fish that are readily available to us — conger eel, crawfish, cod, dogfish, hake, sea bream, mussels and scampi (most firm fish can be used). The stew does not take long to cook and it is best to prepare the accompanying dishes first: rouille, ailloli and toasted bread.

rouille: 2 crushed cloves garlic
2 chillis
1 thick slice bread
stock
3 tbsp olive oil

ailloli: 3 crushed cloves garlic
salt and pepper
2 oz ground hazelnuts
1 egg yolk
$\frac{1}{4}$ pint olive oil
little lemon juice

toasted bread: 8 slices French bread
olive oil

stew: 3 lb mixed fish (see above)
olive oil
1 large onion
1 leek
1 crushed clove garlic
4 tomatoes, skinned and chopped
small bunch parsley
little fresh fennel
pinch saffron

cayenne pepper
2 potatoes, peeled and sliced
$2\frac{1}{2}$ pints water

For the rouille: pound the crushed garlic with the chillis. Remove the crusts from the bread and dip the bread into the stock. Squeeze out the bread and add to the garlic and chilli. Gradually beat in the oil and a little stock to give a smooth paste.

For the ailloli: pound the garlic and seasoning with the nuts. Beat in the egg yolk and gradually add the oil. Add a little lemon juice.

For the toasted bread: dip the bread into olive oil. Put onto a baking sheet and bake in a moderate oven until crisp and golden.

For the stew: clean the fish. Crawfish tails, scampi and mussels are left whole. Cut the large fish, including cod, into large pieces. Put 4 tbsp oil into a large, deep casserole. Add the chopped onion and leek, crushed garlic, tomato, herbs, saffron and cayenne. Add the firm pieces of fish, the potato and water. Bring to the boil and boil for 5 minutes. Add the crawfish and boil for a further 5 minutes. Add the prawns and mussels and boil for a further 5 minutes. Remove the fish and potatoes to a hot serving dish. Split the shells of the crawfish tails, but leave the mussels and prawns in their shells. Taste the soup and correct the seasoning. Boil the soup briskly and strain into a hot tureen. Serve immediately with the fish and potatoes, the toasted bread and the sauces.

(American: fish according to availability, 4 tbsp hazelnuts, $\frac{1}{2}$ cup olive oil, 5 cups water)

* Fish burgers

Serves 4
$\frac{3}{4}$ lb white fish (cod, coley, etc)
1 grated onion
seasoning
3 oz breadcrumbs
grated rind $\frac{1}{2}$ lemon
1 teasp mixed herbs
1 egg
melted butter or oil

Poach or steam the fish until tender. Flake the fish while still warm, discarding any skin and bone. Mix the flaked fish with the onion, seasoning, breadcrumbs, lemon rind, herbs and egg. Form into 4 burgers. Chill for 1 hour. Brush with melted butter or oil and grill for 10 minutes on each side. Serve as a main course with salad and vegetables, or as a snack sandwiched between toasted baps or rolls.

Freeze uncooked.
(American: 1$\frac{1}{2}$ cups fish, 6 tbsp breadcrumbs)

Fish goujons with asparagus and mushroom sauce

Serves 4–6
1$\frac{1}{2}$ lb white fish fillet (cod, plaice, etc)
seasoned flour
beaten egg
dried breadcrumbs
grated rind and juice of 1 lemon
$\frac{1}{4}$ lb button mushrooms, sliced
1 oz butter
1 small can green asparagus tips
$\frac{1}{2}$ pint white sauce (see p 60)
4 tbsp double cream
seasoning
oil for deep frying
lemon sections

Cut the fish into strips, about 3in by $\frac{1}{2}$in. Dust in seasoned flour, dip into beaten egg and then coat evenly with a mixture of crumbs and lemon rind. Simmer the mushrooms in lemon juice and butter until tender. Blend the asparagus and its juice in a liquidizer or push through a sieve. Combine the asparagus puree, white sauce, cream, seasoning and mushrooms. Deep fry the fish goujons in hot oil until crisp and golden. Drain on absorbent paper. Heat the sauce gently. Pile the goujons on to an oval platter and serve with the sauce and sections of lemon.

(American: 2$\frac{1}{4}$ cups fish, $\frac{2}{3}$ cup mushrooms, 2 tbsp butter, 1 cup white sauce)

*Savoury spinach and fish pie

Serves 6
butter
1 lb cooked cod or haddock
½ lb packet frozen spinach, cooked
3 tbsp grated Parmesan cheese
3 tbsp breadcrumbs
1 egg
1 egg yolk
salt and cayenne pepper
grated rind ½ lemon
1 lb potatoes, peeled and thinly
 sliced
¼ pint single cream

Butter a large oval ovenproof dish.
Flake the fish and mix with the
spinach, Parmesan cheese, breadcrumbs, egg, egg yolk, seasoning
and lemon rind. Arrange a layer of
overlapping potato slices in the
bottom of the dish. Top with the fish
and spinach mixture. Cover with a
further layer of overlapping potato
slices. Pour over the cream and dot
the surface generously with butter.
Bake at 375°F, Mark 5, for 1 hour.

(American: 1½ cups fish, ¾ cup
spinach, 2 cups sliced potato, ½ cup
cream)

*Fish goulash

Serves 6
6 small cod cutlets
1½ oz butter
2 onions, sliced
1 tbsp paprika
1 oz plain flour
½ pint stock
½ pint milk
2 tbsp tomato puree
3 tomatoes, skinned and chopped
seasoning
3 oz Philadelphia cream cheese or
 similar
2 tbsp milk

Put the cod cutlets into a large,
shallow casserole. Melt the butter in
a separate pan and fry the onion
gently for 4 minutes. Stir in the
paprika and cook for 1 minute. Add
the flour and cook for a further
minute. Gradually stir in the stock
and milk and bring to the boil. Add
the tomato puree, chopped tomato
and seasoning. Bring back to the
boil and simmer for 20 minutes.
Pour the goulash sauce over the fish.
Cover the casserole and cook at
350°F, Mark 4, for 45 minutes.
Cream the cheese until quite soft
and mix with the milk. Drizzle the
cheese mixture over the top of the
goulash just before serving. Serve
with noodles or rice.

(American: 3 tbsp butter, 2 tbsp
flour, 1 cup stock, 1 cup milk, ½ cup
cream cheese)

Cheesy fish bread pudding

Serves 6
8 slices stale bread
butter
¾ lb coley

6 processed Cheddar cheese slices
2 eggs
$\frac{1}{2}$ pint milk
$\frac{1}{4}$ pint double cream
seasoning

Spread the bread generously with butter. Remove the crusts and cut the bread into triangles. Cut the fish into small pieces, discarding any bones and dark skin. Arrange the bread, fish and cheese slices in layers, finishing with a layer of bread. Beat the eggs with the milk, cream and seasoning. Pour over the other ingredients. Bake at 350°F, Mark 4, for 45 minutes. Serve hot. This pudding is particularly good with mustard sauce (see p 60)

(American: 1½ cups fish, 1 cup milk, ½ cup cream)

* Haddock scallops

Serves 6
1 lb haddock fillet
1 lb potatoes
$\frac{3}{4}$ pint white sauce (see p 60)
seasoning
1 tbsp tomato puree
4 oz grated cheese
3 tomatoes

Either grill or poach the fish. Flake the fish while it is still warm. Peel the potatoes and cut into cubes. Cook in boiling salted water until just tender. Drain. Bind the fish and potato with the white sauce and add

the seasoning, tomato puree and 3 oz of the cheese. Spoon into 6 greased scallop shells or individual ovenproof dishes. Top with slices of tomato and the rest of the cheese. Bake at 375°F, Mark 5, for 25 minutes.

(American: 1½ cups haddock, 2 cups cubed potato, 1½ cups white sauce, ½ cup cheese)

Fish in wine and philly sauce

Serves 4
1 lb haddock fillet
1 green pepper
2 oz whole blanched almonds
2 tbsp oil
4 oz Philadelphia cream cheese or similar
1 oz plain flour
$\frac{1}{2}$ pint white wine
$\frac{1}{4}$ pint chicken stock
seasoning

Cut the haddock into strips and put into a shallow ovenproof dish. Remove the core and seeds from the pepper, and chop. Fry the pepper and nuts in the oil until lightly browned, and spoon half over the fish, reserving the rest for garnish. Soften the cream cheese and beat in the flour. Gradually add the wine and stock, beating to avoid lumps forming. Pour the sauce over the fish and add seasoning. Cover the dish and cook at 350°F, Mark 4, for 40 minutes. Spoon the remaining nuts and pepper over the fish before serving.

(American: 1½ cups haddock, 3 tbsp nuts, ⅔ cup cream cheese, 2 tbsp flour, 1 cup wine, ½ cup stock)

*Haddock and Danish blue savoury

Serves 6–8
1 pint packet aspic jelly crystals
½ pint boiling water
4 hard-boiled eggs
4 oz Danish Blue cheese
½ lb haddock, cooked and flaked
¼ pint soured cream
3 tbsp chopped parsley
2 egg whites
seasoning

Put the aspic crystals into a bowl, add the boiling water and stir until dissolved. Push the hard-boiled eggs and the Danish Blue cheese through a coarse sieve. Mix in the flaked fish, soured cream and the cool aspic. Put in a cool place until it is on the point of setting. Whisk the egg whites stiffly and fold into the mixture. Either spoon into a lightly greased loaf tin so that the savoury can be unmoulded when set, or spoon into small individual souffle dishes. Leave to set.

(American: 1 cup boiling water, ½ cup cheese, ¾ cup flaked fish, ½ cup soured cream)

Plaice meuniere

Serves 4
8 small plaice fillets
seasoned flour
3 oz butter
1 tbsp oil
juice ½ lemon
1 tbsp chopped parsley
lemon wedges

Coat the fillets of plaice on both sides in seasoned flour. Heat 2 oz of the butter and the oil in a shallow pan. Add the plaice fillets and fry for 6–8 minutes, turning once, until golden and cooked through. Remove to a serving dish and keep warm. Add the lemon juice, remaining butter and parsley to the fat in the pan and heat through until nutty and golden brown. Pour over the fish, garnish with lemon wedges and serve with tartare sauce (p 61).

(American: 6 tbsp butter)

Plaice aux bananes

Serves 6
2 oz seedless raisins
6 tbsp sweet white wine
3 oz butter
6 large or 12 small plaice fillets
3 bananas
juice of ½ lemon
seasoning
2 oz golden breadcrumbs

Put the raisins into a small bowl with the wine and leave to steep until plumped. Grease a shallow oven-proof dish with a little of the butter. Roll up the plaice fillets and put in the bottom of the dish. Sprinkle with lemon juice and season. Top with the sliced banana, raisins and wine. Dot with remaining butter and scatter with the breadcrumbs. Bake at 375°F, Mark 5, for 25 minutes.

(American: $\frac{1}{4}$ cup raisins, 6 tbsp butter, 3 tbsp breadcrumbs)

Skate in brown butter

Serves 4
2 lb skate
1$\frac{1}{2}$ pints water
5 tbsp wine vinegar
salt and pepper
piece of mace
few parsley stalks
4 oz butter
2 tbsp capers
2 tbsp chopped parsley

Cut the skate into 4 wing pieces, or ask the fishmonger to do it for you. Put the skate into a shallow pan. Add the water, 1 tbsp vinegar, 1 teasp salt, the mace and parlsey stalks. Bring to the boil and simmer for 12–15 minutes, until fish is tender. Remove the skate, draining thoroughly, and carefully remove the skin. Keep warm in a serving dish. Put the remaining vinegar into a pan and boil rapidly until reduced by half. Add the butter and heat until it is browned but not burnt.

Stir in the capers, parsley and seasoning. Pour over the fish and serve immediately.

(American: 4 medium wing pieces of skate, 3 cups water, $\frac{1}{2}$ cup butter)

Paupiettes of sole with Dutch lettuce stuffing

Serves 6
12 small sole fillets
2 small Dutch lettuce
2 hard-boiled eggs
4 oz peeled prawns
seasoning
grated rind and juice of 1 lemon
1 tbsp double cream
butter
$\frac{3}{4}$ pint dry white wine
2 egg yolks
$\frac{1}{4}$ pint double cream
1 large red pepper
2 tbsp chopped parsley
few unpeeled prawns

Remove the outer leaves from the lettuce. Wash, dry and shred finely, and reserve for the garnish. Separate the heart lettuce leaves and wash and dry. Place two to three heart lettuce leaves on each fish fillet. Mix the chopped hard-boiled egg with the chopped prawns, seasoning, lemon rind and 1 tbsp cream. Divide the mixture amongst the fish fillets. Roll up carefully, enclosing the lettuce and the stuffing. Secure with wooden cocktail sticks. Butter a large shallow ovenproof dish. Place fish in the dish and add the wine. Cover with a circle of buttered paper. Cook at 375°F, Mark 5 for 25–30 minutes, until fish is just tender. Remove fish from the liquid and keep warm. Mix the egg yolks with the cream. Add to the cooking liquid and heat through to thicken, but do not boil. Mix the shredded lettuce with the pepper cut into thin strips, and toss in lemon juice and chopped parsley. Arrange the paupiettes in the centre of a serving dish with the lettuce and pepper around the edge. Spoon the sauce over the fish and garnish with prawns. Serve with asparagus tips and croquette potatoes.

(American: $\frac{2}{3}$ cup peeled prawns, $1\frac{1}{2}$ cups dry white wine, $\frac{1}{2}$ cup cream)

Baked sole knots

Serves 6
6 large sole fillets
1 onion, finely chopped
3 oz butter
6 tomatoes, skinned, seeded and chopped
6 anchovy fillets, chopped
6 oz button mushrooms
seasoning

Cut the sole fillets into thin strips, approximately 5in by $\frac{1}{2}$in. Place in the base of a greased shallow oven-proof dish. Fry the onion gently in the butter for 5 minutes. Add the chopped tomato and cook for 3 minutes. Add the anchovy fillets, mushrooms and seasoning. Spoon over the fish. Bake at 375°F, Mark 5, for 20–25 minutes, until the fish is just tender.

(American: 6 tbsp butter, $1\frac{1}{4}$ cups mushrooms)

Whiting with lemon and mint

Serves 4
4 small whiting, cleaned
seasoning
1 onion
3 large sprigs of mint
1 lemon
bay leaf
$\frac{1}{2}$ pint white wine

Ease the whiting open and season inside and out. Put the sliced onion, mint, lemon cut into slices, and bay leaf into a roasting tin large enough to take the rack from your grill pan. Put the rack into the tin and place the fish on top. Pour over the wine and add sufficient water so that the level of the liquid comes just under the fish. Cover with a lid or with a piece of foil. Cook at 300°F, Mark 2, for $1\frac{1}{4}$ hours. (The excess cooking liquid makes a good base for a fish soup.) Serve with maitre d'hotel sauce (see p 60).

(American: 1 cup white wine)

Oily fish

The oily fish group includes the herring family: pilchards, sardines, sprats, whitebait, and of course the herring itself, the most common type. Mackerel and red and grey mullet are not as well known as herring but they are available from most fishmongers.

All oily fish are very nutritious, being rich in vitamin D and mineral salts. Sardines in particular are very rich in fluorine, which helps prevent tooth decay. Oily fish have a high fat content and so they are satisfying; but they are not a good choice for small children and invalids since they are not easily digestible.

Herring, pilchards and sardines are available virtually the whole year round. Mackerel, red mullet and whitebait are best during the spring and summer months. Grey mullet and sprats are most readily available in late autumn and winter.

Berlin herrings

Serves 4
4 large herrings
seasoning
good pinch powdered mace
4 cloves
6 crushed black peppercorns
1 bay leaf
1 onion, thinly sliced
¼ pint malt vinegar
¼ pint apple juice
¾ lb cooking apples, peeled, cored
    and sliced
juice of 1 lemon
1 tbsp brown sugar
1 teasp mixed spice
pinch ground ginger
pinch ground nutmeg

Scale and clean the herrings. Remove
the heads and tails. Split each one in
half and remove the bones. Season
the flat fillets with salt and pepper,
and roll up from the tail end, with
the skin outside. Put the herrings
into a small shallow ovenproof dish.
Add the spices, bay leaf and onion,
and pour over the vinegar and apple
juice. Cover the dish and bake at
350°F, Mark 4, for 45 minutes.
Meanwhile make the sauce: put the
apple into a pan with the lemon
juice, sugar and spices. Cover and
simmer gently until the apple is
tender. Sieve. Serve the herrings and
sauce hot or cold.

(American: ½ cup malt vinegar, ½
cup apple juice, 1 cup cooked apple)

Herrings with mustard cream

Serves 4
4 herrings
melted butter
seasoning
¼ pint double cream
1 dessertsp made mustard
2 teasp vinegar
3 tbsp bottled Coleslaw Dressing
1 small onion, grated

Clean the herrings, and remove the
heads and tails. Brush the herrings
with melted butter and season. Grill
for 6–8 minutes on either side, until
just tender. Meanwhile make the
mustard cream: lightly whip the
cream. Mix with the mustard,
vinegar, Coleslaw Dressing, grated
onion and seasoning. Garnish the
cooked herrings with wedges of
lemon and serve with the mustard
cream.

(American: ½ cup double cream)

Quick matelote normande

Serves 4
2 herrings, cleaned and cut into
    pieces
2 mullet, cleaned and cut into pieces
2 oz butter
3 tbsp brandy or whisky
½ pint dry cider
⅓ pint stock
seasoning

1 tbsp chopped chives
¼ lb button mushrooms
2 egg yolks
5 tbsp cream

Cook the fish in the butter until it colours lightly (pale golden). Pour over the brandy or whisky and very carefully set light to it. Stir the fish about until the flames die down. Add the cider, stock, seasoning, chives and mushrooms. Simmer gently for about 20–25 minutes, until the fish is just tender. Beat the egg yolks with the cream and mix with a little of the hot fish liquid. Add to the fish in the pan and stir over a gentle heat until lightly thickened. Do not allow to boil. Serve with quick garlic bread (see p 26).

Variation: add a few shelled cooked mussels to the matelote.

(American: ¼ cup butter, ⅔ cup mushrooms)

*Jansonn's herrings

Serves 4

This is a tasty alternative to the traditional Jansonn's temptation, and makes a very pleasant substantial supper dish.

1½ lb potatoes
1 onion, sliced
2 oz butter
½ pint single cream
seasoning

4 herrings
1 can anchovy fillets
chopped parsley

Peel the potatoes. Slice and cut into very thin strips. Put into a greased ovenproof dish with the onion. Dot with butter and pour over half the cream. Season. Bake at 400°F, Mark 6, for 20 minutes. Clean the herrings and remove the heads and tails. Lay on top of the potato. Drain the anchovy fillets and pour the oil over the herrings. Spoon over the remaining cream. Make a lattice with the anchovy fillets. Continue baking for a further ½ hour. Sprinkle with chopped parsley and serve with a crisp salad.

(American: 3 cups potato strips, ¼ cup butter, 1 cup cream)

Soft roes a la creme

Serves 4
¾ lb soft herring roes
seasoned flour
2 oz butter
1 crushed clove garlic
½ pint cream
2 tbsp chopped parsley
juice ½ lemon
plain boiled rice

Rinse the roes in cold water. Drain on absorbent paper and dust lightly in seasoned flour. Heat the butter with the crushed garlic. Add the soft roes and fry gently for 4 minutes, turning once or twice. Add the cream and parsley and bring just to the boil. Sprinkle with lemon juice and serve immediately with the boiled rice.

(American: a generous cup soft herring roes, ¼ cup butter, 1 cup cream)

Mackerel by moonlight

Serves 4
4 small mackerel
juice 1 lemon
3 oz butter
seasoning
½ lb tomatoes, skinned and chopped
1 crushed clove garlic
1 red pepper, seeded and sliced
1 green pepper, seeded and sliced
lemon slices

Clean the mackerel. Place on a large piece of greased foil. Sprinkle with lemon juice, dot with butter and season. Fold the foil over the fish to enclose them completely. Bake at 375°F, Mark 5, for 45 minutes. Meanwhile make the sauce: melt 1 oz of the butter. Add the crushed garlic, tomatoes and peppers. Simmer gently until soft. Arrange the cooked mackerel on a serving dish and spoon over the hot sauce. Garnish with lemon slices.

(American: 6 tbsp butter, ¾ cup chopped tomatoes)

Mackerel savoie

Serves 4
4 medium size mackerel
½ cucumber, thinly sliced
¼ pint dry white wine
2 oz butter
seasoning
3 oz chopped walnuts
¼ pint double cream
4 teasp caster sugar
1 tbsp creamed horseradish

Clean the mackerel. Remove the heads and tails. Place the cucumber in a shallow greased ovenproof dish. Lay the mackerel on top. Pour over the wine and dot with butter. Season to taste. Bake at 375°F, Mark 5, for about 40 minutes, until the fish is just tender. Meanwhile make the walnut and horseradish sauce: chop the walnuts finely. Mix with the double cream, sugar, creamed horseradish and seasoning. Serve with the fish.

(American: ½ cup white wine, ¼ cup butter, ⅓ cup chopped walnuts, ½ cup double cream)

Mackerel maltaise

Serves 4
4 mackerel
grated rind 1 orange (see recipe)
grated rind 1 lemon (see recipe)
3 tbsp white wine vinegar
1 tbsp oil
1 tbsp sugar

seasoning
3 tbsp marmalade

Clean the mackerel. The heads may be removed or left on, as you prefer. Put the fish into a shallow ovenproof dish. Add the grated fruit rinds, wine vinegar, oil, sugar and seasoning. Cover the dish and leave to marinate in the refrigerator overnight. Strain off the liquid from the fish into a saucepan. Add the marmalade and stir over the heat until dissolved. Spoon the marmalade sauce over the fish. Cover the dish and cook at 375°F, Mark 5, for 45 minutes. Serve either hot or chilled. The citrus flavour of the sauce is quite strong. If you like something less pungent, reduce the amount of lemon and orange rind.

Skewered mackerel

Serves 4
4 small mackerel
8 bay leaves
20 small mushrooms
8 rashers bacon, rolled
seasoning
juice ½ lemon
1 teasp mixed herbs
6 tbsp olive oil

Ask the fishmonger to remove the backbones from the mackerel for you. Cut each fish through into 6 pieces. Thread the pieces of mackerel on to 4 long skewers, alternating them with bay leaves, mushrooms and bacon rolls. Put into a shallow dish. Season, sprinkle with lemon juice and herbs, and spoon over the oil. Cover the dish and chill for 2 hours. Put the skewers under the grill and cook for 12 minutes, turning them from time to time. Serve with a mixed salad and mustard sauce (see p 60).

Italian baked mullet

Serves 4
4 medium size mullet
seasoning
2 oz grated cheese
2 oz butter
6 tbsp white wine
6 oz pasta shells
grated rind ½ lemon
2 tbsp chopped parsley

Clean and wash the mullet. Place in a greased ovenproof dish. Season and sprinkle with grated cheese. Dot the surface with butter. Spoon over the wine. Cover with greased greaseproof paper and bake at 400°F, Mark 6, for 20 minutes. Remove the paper and return to the oven for a further 10 minutes. Meanwhile cook the pasta shells in boiling salted water for about 8 minutes, until just tender. Drain in a colander. Heat a little butter in a pan. Add the pasta shells, lemon rind and chopped parsley and season well. Just before serving, spoon the pasta around the fish. (American: $\frac{1}{4}$ cup grated cheese, $\frac{1}{4}$ cup butter, 1 cup pasta shells)

Spanish-style mullet

Serves 4
4 mullet
6 tbsp breadcrumbs
3 oz stuffed Spanish olives
1 teasp oregano
1 tbsp chopped parsley
3 spring onions, finely chopped
1 tbsp oil
1 egg yolk
seasoning
2 oz butter
grated rind $\frac{1}{2}$ lemon

Clean and scale the mullet. Mix the breadcrumbs with half the chopped Spanish olives, oregano, parsley, spring onions, oil, egg yolk and seasoning. Spoon the stuffing into the cavity of each mullet. Place in an ovenproof dish. Heat the butter with the remaining olives. Add the lemon rind and pour over fish. Bake at 375°F, Mark 5, for 30–35 minutes.

(American: $\frac{1}{3}$ cup stuffed Spanish olives, $\frac{1}{4}$ cup butter)

Stargazey pie

Serves 6
No cookery book featuring oily fish would be complete without a recipe for this Cornish speciality—there have been many recipes handed down over the years, but this is one of the tastiest and easiest to serve.

1 lb shortcrust pastry
6 fresh pilchards (alternatively use medium size herrings or large, fresh sardines)
seasoning
1 small onion, finely chopped
1 teasp mixed herbs
4 oz streaky bacon, chopped
2 hard-boiled eggs, chopped
saffron milk

Roll out half the pastry and use to line a large greased pie plate or shallow ovenproof dish. Ask the fishmonger to gut and bone the pilchards for you, leaving the heads on. Season the fish inside with salt, pepper, onion and herbs. Fold fish back into shape. Arrange the fish on the pastry so that the heads lie evenly around the rim. Sprinkle with chopped bacon and hard-boiled egg. Roll out the remaining pastry and cut a circle large enough to cover the fish, leaving the heads exposed. Place over the pilchards and press pastry down between each one. Brush with saffron milk. Bake at 400°F, Mark 6, for 30 minutes, then reduce heat to 350°F, Mark 4, for a further 15 minutes.

For saffron milk: soak a pinch of powdered saffron in a little warm milk.

(American: 2 cups shortcrust pastry, ½ cup chopped streaky bacon)

Simply sardines

Serves 4
8 medium size sardines
oil
juice ½ lemon
seasoning
1 teasp dill seed
4 tbsp Thousand Island dressing
   (bottled)
1 lemon

Place the sardines in a shallow ovenproof dish. Pour over a little oil, just sufficient to moisten, and season to taste. Put under a moderately hot grill and grill until lightly golden. Turn the sardines carefully. Sprinkle with lemon juice and dill seed and spoon over the Thousand Island dressing. Continue grilling the sardines until they are just tender. Serve hot, garnished with wedges of lemon.

Sardines shashlik

Serves 4
12 medium size fresh sardines
flour
beaten egg
fine breadcrumbs
9 thin rashers streaky bacon
4 oz butter
2 hard-boiled eggs, chopped
2 tbsp chopped parsley

Clean the sardines. Remove the heads and tails. Cut each sardine in half widthways. Dust in flour. Dip into beaten egg and coat evenly in crumbs. Cut the bacon rashers in half and wrap one piece around each half sardine. Thread six pieces on to each skewer (using 4 skewers in all). Cook under a moderately hot grill for about 8 minutes, turning once. For the sauce: heat the butter until foaming. Add the chopped hard-boiled egg and the parsley and heat through. Serve the sauce with the grilled shashlik.

(American: ½ cup butter)

Devilled sprats

Serves 4
1 lb sprats
2–3 oz seasoned flour
2 teasp dry mustard
cayenne pepper
oil for deep frying

Wash the sprats and gut them through the gills, leaving the heads intact. Dry them carefully on a clean cloth. Put the seasoned flour into a plastic bag with the dry mustard and 1 teasp cayenne pepper. Add the sprats and shake the bag until they are evenly coated. Deep fry in hot oil for about 3 minutes. Drain well. Sprinkle with extra cayenne pepper and serve immediately with wedges of lemon, brown bread and butter, and curry sauce (see p 60).

(American: approximately 3 cups sprats)

(American: approximately 3 cups whitebait, 1½ cups canned tomatoes)

Whitebait provencal

Serves 4

This makes a very pleasant change to the more traditional fried whitebait. The advantage with these tiny fish is that there is no fiddly preparation. You eat the whole fish, including the head and the tail.

1 lb whitebait
1 onion, chopped
2 crushed cloves garlic
2 tbsp oil
14 oz can tomatoes
2 tbsp tomato puree
1 teasp sugar
1 teasp chopped dried basil
chopped parsley

Rinse the whitebait in cold water and drain. Fry the onion and garlic gently in oil for 5 minutes. Add the canned tomatoes, tomato puree, sugar and basil. Simmer gently for 20 minutes. Add the whitebait and simmer gently for a further 5 minutes. Either serve hot with garlic bread or leave to become quite cold and serve with brown bread and butter.

For quick garlic bread: dip slices of stale French bread into bottled Italian Garlic Dressing, and toast or bake until golden.

Whitebait au gratin

Serves 4

¾ lb whitebait
¼ pint soured cream
¼ pint double cream
seasoning
grated rind ½ lemon
2 oz grated cheese

Divide the washed and dried whitebait between four greased individual ovenproof dishes. Mix the creams with the seasoning and grated lemon rind. Spoon evenly over the whitebait. Sprinkle the tops with grated cheese. Bake at 375°F, Mark 5, for 20 minutes. Serve with fingers of hot toast.

(American: 2¼ cups whitebait, ½ cup soured cream, ½ cup double cream, ¼ cup grated cheese)

Freshwater fish

Freshwater fish fall into two categories: those that live permanently in rivers, lakes and streams, such as bream, carp, eel, perch, pike and trout, and those that are partly sea fish, spending their early lives in the sea and then returning to the rivers when fully developed, such as salmon and salmon trout. Carp, bream, eel and trout are the most readily available of the true freshwater fish. British anglers tend to throw other varieties back.

The secret with freshwater fish is to cook them as freshly as possible. Most freshwater fish is best poached or baked. Whichever method you choose, ensure that the fish is kept moist.

Bream, salmon and salmon trout are best during the spring and summer months, whereas the other freshwater fish are better during the autumn and winter months.

Bream napolitaine

Serves 4

1 bream weighing about 2–2½ lb
seasoning
1 onion, chopped
1 crushed clove garlic
1½ oz butter
2 tbsp oil
1 green pepper, seeded and cut into
  strips
14 oz can tomatoes
2 tbsp tomato puree
1 teasp sugar
½ teasp dried oregano
cooked spaghetti or noodles

Cut the bream into 4 thick cutlets
(if you ask the fishmonger he will do
this for you). Put the cutlets into a
greased shallow ovenproof dish and
season. Fry the onion and garlic in
the butter and oil for 4 minutes. Add
the pepper and fry for a further 3
minutes. Add the canned tomatoes,
tomato puree, sugar and oregano.
Simmer for 5 minutes. Pour the
sauce over the bream. Cover the
dish and cook at 350°F, Mark 4,
for 30–35 minutes. Serve on a bed
of noodles or spaghetti.

(American: 1 medium size bream,
3 tbsp butter, 1½ cups tomatoes)

Carp with mock caviare

Serves 4–6

1 carp weighing about 2½ lb
2 onions, sliced
1 bay leaf
1 teasp crushed peppercorns
1 teasp salt
1 teasp mixed dried herbs
½ pint white wine
¼ pint mayonnaise (see p 60)
grated rind ½ lemon
small jar lumpfish roe
lemon slices
parsley

Gut and clean the fish. Wash in
salted water. Place the fish on the
rack of a fish kettle (or on a rack
inside a deep oval casserole). Add
the onion, bay leaf, peppercorns,
salt, herbs, wine and sufficient water
to come halfway up the sides of the
fish. Cover the fish kettle and
simmer very gently for 30–35
minutes until the fish is tender.
Allow the fish to cool slightly before
removing it. Carefully lift the carp
on to a serving dish, and remove the
top skin. Put the mayonnaise into a
pan with the lemon rind and 5 tbsp
of the strained poaching liquid.
Simmer for 2–3 minutes. Stir in the
lumpfish roe. Garnish the carp with
lemon slices and sprigs of parsley,
and serve with the sauce.

(American: a medium size carp, or
similar fish, 1 cup white wine, ½ cup
mayonnaise)

Carpe au vin rouge

Serves 4
2½ lb carp
1 onion, chopped
4 oz mushrooms, sliced
3 oz currants
2 crushed cloves garlic
bay leaf
sprig thyme
1¼ pints red wine
seasoning
2 oz butter
1 oz flour
croutons

Clean the carp. Remove the head and the tail and cut the body into pieces. Put the onion, mushrooms, currants, garlic, bay leaf and thyme into a pan with the red wine and seasoning. Simmer for about ½ hour, until reduced by ⅓. Add the carp to the pan. Cover and continue cooking for a further ½ hour. Cream the butter and flour together. Add to the pan, in small pieces, beating until well blended with the liquid. Heat through to thicken. Serve with fried bread croutons.

(American: ⅔ cup mushrooms, ½ cup currants, 2½ cups red wine, ¼ cup butter, 2 tbsp flour)

Jellied eels

Serves 4
2 lb freshwater eel
1½ pints water
4 tbsp vinegar
2 teasp salt
1 bay leaf
small bunch parsley stalks
1 teasp crushed peppercorns
1 carrot, sliced
1 onion, sliced

Skin and clean the eel (if the skin appears to be very tough leave it on and remove after cooking). Cut the eel into ¾ in thick slices. Put the water, vinegar, salt, bay leaf, parsley stalks, peppercorns, carrot and onion into a pan. Bring to the boil and simmer for 25 minutes. Strain the liquid and return to the pan. Add the eel to the liquid and simmer gently for 15 minutes. Remove the eel from the pan and discard the bones. Boil the liquid rapidly until it is reduced by one third. Put the eel into a dish and pour the liquid over. Cool, and then chill until a jelly forms. Serve with brown bread and butter.

(American: buy eel according to its size, 3 cups water)

Matelote of eel

Serves 4
2 lb eel, skinned and cut into short
    lengths
4 tbsp brandy
7 tbsp oil
seasoning

6 oz dried prunes
$\frac{3}{4}$ pint white wine
1 onion, chopped
3 rashers streaky bacon, chopped
$\frac{1}{4}$ lb button mushrooms
2 egg yolks
4 tbsp double cream
triangles of toast

Put the eel into a shallow dish and add brandy, 4 tbsp oil and seasoning. Cover and leave in the refrigerator overnight. Soak the prunes in wine overnight. Fry the onion and bacon in the remaining 3 tbsp oil for 5 minutes. Add the drained pieces of eel and fry until lightly browned. Add the mushrooms, the marinating liquor from the eel and the prunes and wine. Simmer for 30 minutes. Mix the egg yolks with the cream and blend with a little of the hot eel liquid. Add the egg and cream to the pan and stir over a gentle heat until thickened. Do not boil. Serve hot with triangles of toast.

(American: 2 medium size eels, $\frac{3}{4}$ cup prunes, $1\frac{1}{2}$ cups white wine, $\frac{2}{3}$ cup button mushrooms)

Eel meuniere with brandy sauce

Serves 6
24 eel fillets (see recipe)
seasoned flour
4 oz butter
juice $\frac{1}{2}$ lemon

sauce:
1 oz butter
1 small onion, finely chopped
$\frac{3}{4}$ oz flour
$\frac{1}{4}$ pint stock
$\frac{1}{2}$ pint white wine
3 oz button mushrooms, sliced
3 tbsp brandy
seasoning

Ask your fishmonger to cut the eel either into fillets or into long diagonal slices. Toss the eel fillets in seasoned flour. Melt the butter in a shallow pan and fry the eel fillets until tender and golden. Sprinkle with lemon juice and keep warm.

For the sauce: fry the chopped onion in butter for 4 minutes. Stir in the flour and cook for 1 minute. Add the stock and white wine gradually. Bring to the boil, add the sliced mushrooms and simmer for 5 minutes. Stir in the brandy and adjust seasoning to taste. Serve the eel fillets on an oval platter, masked with the sauce and garnished with small puff pastry cases filled with Patum Pepperium (anchovy paste).

(American: $\frac{1}{2}$ cup butter, 2 tbsp butter, $1\frac{1}{2}$ tbsp flour, $\frac{1}{2}$ cup stock, 1 cup wine, $\frac{1}{2}$ cup mushrooms)

Herbed perch fillets

Serves 6
12 perch fillets
$\frac{1}{4}$ pt olive oil

juice 1 lemon
1 small onion, finely chopped
seasoning
flour
beaten egg
breadcrumbs
3 oz butter
2 teasp chopped dried sage

Put the perch fillets into a shallow dish with 7 tbsp of the oil, the lemon juice, onion and seasoning. Cover and leave in the refrigerator for 2 hours. Drain perch fillets well. Dip in flour, then beaten egg and coat evenly with breadcrumbs. Heat 3 oz of the butter with the remaining tbsp oil. Add the perch and fry until nicely browned. Keep warm on a serving dish. Add remaining 1 oz of butter to the pan with 2 tbsp of the fish marinade and the sage. Heat through until bubbling. Pour over the perch and serve immediately.

(American: ½ cup olive oil, 6 tbsp butter)

Pike quenelles

Serves 4
¾ lb pike (free from skin and bone)
seasoning
good pinch grated nutmeg
2 tbsp chopped parsley
2 egg whites
¼ pint double cream
½ pint stock (preferably fish)
½ pint white wine

Mince the fish finely. Pound with the seasoning, nutmeg and parsley and press through a sieve. Stand the basin containing the fish mixture in a larger bowl of ice and leave to stiffen for about an hour. Work in the chilled cream gradually, still keeping the bowl over ice. Mould into egg shapes, using 2 tablespoons dipped in hot water, and put into a shallow greased pan. Leave a space between each quenelle as they swell during cooking. Bring the stock and wine to the boil and pour over the quenelles. Poach gently until the quenelles puff up and feel firm. Lift out of the pan carefully with a slotted spoon and serve immediately with chantilly or hollandaise sauce (see p 61).

(American: 1¼ cups pike flesh, ½ cup double cream, 1 cup stock, 1 cup white wine)

Simple salmon

Serves 4
4 salmon cutlets, cut 1 in thick
grated rind ½ lemon
2 tbsp chopped parsley
seasoning
bay leaf
½ pint single cream

Put the salmon cutlets into a greased shallow ovenproof dish. Sprinkle with the grated lemon rind, parsley and seasoning. Add the bay leaf and pour over the cream. Bake at 375°F, Mark 5, for 20–25 minutes, until the fish is just tender. Baste with cream once or twice during the cooking.

(American: 1 cup cream)

*Salmon en croute

Serves 4
4 small salmon cutlets
seasoning
butter
2 teasp chopped fresh tarragon
few drops Tabasco
grated rind $\frac{1}{2}$ lemon
1$\frac{1}{2}$ lb puff pastry
beaten egg
egg sauce (see p 60)
cucumber salad

Season the salmon cutlets. Put into the grill pan and dot the surface with butter. Grill for 3 minutes. Turn the cutlets and grill for a further 3 minutes. Allow to cool. Soften 3 oz butter. Add the tarragon, Tabasco, lemon rind and seasoning. Roll out puff pastry thinly. Using a small oval pie dish as a guide, cut 8 oval shapes from the pastry. Brush the edges of 4 of the pastry shapes with beaten egg. Place a parcooked salmon cutlet into the centre of each. Spread the top of the cutlets generously with the flavoured butter. Lay the remaining pastry shapes over the fish. Pinch the pastry edges together to seal and completely enclose the fish. Notch decoratively. Place on a greased baking sheet and glaze with beaten egg. Bake at 400°F, Mark 6, for 35–40 minutes. Serve with egg sauce and cucumber salad.

Freeze unbaked.

(American: 3 cups puff pastry)

Fish chantilly

Serves 4
1 thick cutlet salmon (weighing about 10 oz)
$\frac{1}{4}$ pint white wine
seasoning
bay leaf
$\frac{1}{2}$ small cucumber, sliced thinly
1 lettuce heart, shredded
grated rind and juice 1 orange
2 tbsp chopped parsley
1 orange, peeled, depipped and chopped
4 tbsp oil
$\frac{1}{4}$ pint mayonnaise (see p 60)
4 tbsp double cream
1 oz flaked almonds, toasted

Put the salmon into a small shallow pan. Add the wine, seasoning and bay leaf. Cover with a circle of buttered greaseproof paper and poach gently until the salmon is just tender—about 15 minutes. Cool. Remove skin and bone and flake the salmon. Mix the cucumber, lettuce, orange rind, parsley and chopped orange. Combine the orange juice, oil and seasoning, and lightly toss the salad vegetables and orange in the dressing. Spoon into glass cocktail dishes. Arrange the flaked salmon on top. Mix the cream with the mayonnaise and spoon over the fish. Scatter with toasted nuts.

(American: 1 cup flaked salmon, $\frac{1}{2}$ cup white wine, $\frac{1}{2}$ cup mayonnaise, 2 tbsp nuts)

Salmon trout Beau Monde

Serves 6
$\frac{1}{2}$ lb fish trimmings
1 onion, sliced
1 carrot, peeled and sliced
bay leaf
sprig tarragon
olive oil
$\frac{2}{3}$ pint Beau Monde*
seasoning
1 onion, chopped
3 oz mushrooms, chopped
2 oz butter
3 tbsp chopped parsley
2$\frac{1}{4}$ lb salmon trout, cleaned
1 lemon, thinly sliced

Put the fish trimmings, onion, carrot, bay leaf, tarragon, 2 tbsp olive oil, Beau Monde and seasoning into a pan. Bring to the boil and simmer gently for $\frac{1}{2}$ hour. Allow to cool and then strain the fish stock. Fry the chopped onion and mushrooms in butter for 10 minutes. Stir in the chopped parsley and seasoning. Stuff the salmon trout with the mixture. Place on a sheet of foil large enough to enclose the complete fish. Top with the sliced lemon and spoon over 6 tbsp fish stock and 4 tbsp olive oil. Freeze any remaining stock or store it in the refrigerator for up to 1 week. Fold the foil over to enclose the fish and seal. Place the foil parcel on a flat baking sheet. Cook at 375°F, Mark 5, for 25–30 minutes, until fish is just tender. Allow the fish to cool in its package. Then carefully remove to a serving dish. Garnish with lemon and parsley and serve with buttered new potatoes and a selection of salads.

Beau Monde can only be obtained from one supplier in this country, W E Tucker Ltd, Sudbury, Suffolk. It gives the best results for this recipe, but another sparkling white wine can be used.

(American: 1 cup fish trimmings, 1$\frac{1}{4}$ cups Beau Monde, $\frac{1}{2}$ cup mushrooms, $\frac{1}{4}$ cup butter)

Trout vinaigrette

Serves 4
This is a traditional German way of serving trout and a well chilled Mosel wine makes an ideal accompaniment to the fish.

4 medium size trout
2 oz butter
1 onion, thinly sliced
1 small green pepper, finely chopped
1 hard-boiled egg, chopped

4 tbsp cream
4 teasp wine vinegar
seasoning

Clean the trout. Melt the butter in a large frying pan. Add the onion and pepper and fry gently for 5 minutes. Remove from the pan. Add the trout to the pan and fry gently for about 6 minutes on each side, until golden brown. Remove the trout and put it on a serving dish. Fry the chopped egg for 1 minute in the remaining butter. Add the cream, wine vinegar and fried pepper and onion. Season to taste. Heat through. Spoon the sauce over the fish and serve.

(American: $\frac{1}{4}$ cup butter)

Trout gourmet

Serves 4
1 large uncut white loaf
butter
4 medium size trout
seasoning
5 tbsp sherry
4 oz chicken liver pate (smooth)

Cut 2 slices about $\frac{1}{2}$in thick lengthways from the loaf. This is all you will need for the recipe, but the rest of the loaf is still quite usable. Remove the crusts from the slices and cut each in half lengthways. Spread generously with butter. Put the trout into a shallow ovenproof dish. Dot with butter, season, and spoon the sherry over the fish. Cook the trout at 375°F, Mark 5 for 25–30 minutes. Bake the buttered bread in the oven at the same time. Spread the toasted bread with pate and put onto a serving dish. Place a trout on top of each, and spoon over the cooking juices.

(American: $\frac{1}{2}$ cup pate)

Trout on twigs

Serves 4
dried fennel stalks
4 trout
melted butter
seasoning
3 tbsp brandy

The fish can be cooked in the grill pan, but it is better and more convenient to use a shallow ovenproof dish which is large enough to take the rack from your grill pan. Put sufficient fennel stalks into the base of a shallow ovenproof dish (or the grill pan), to make a thin layer. Put the rack over the top and lay the trout on the rack. Brush with melted butter and season. Grill for about 7 minutes. Turn the fish and grill for a further 6 minutes. Heat the brandy in a ladle. Carefully set light to it, and spoon immediately over the fish and fennel. Let the fennel catch fire so that the aroma scents the fish. (Do not worry—the flames will die down very quickly!)

Smoked fish

Smoked fish ranges from the expensive types like smoked salmon to the more economical smoked fish such as kipper and bloater. The whole smoked fish family consists of the following: bloater, buckling, smoked cod, smoked cod's roe, smoked eel, smoked haddock, kipper, smoked mackerel, smoked salmon, smoked sprats and smoked trout.

Smoking was originally a method of preserving fish when there was a glut. Now many fish are smoked to produce the popular, characteristic flavour. Fish can be smoked either cold or hot. The fish is not cooked in cold smoking, but with hot smoking it is lightly cooked. Hot smoked fish such as mackerel are richer in flavour than cold smoked fish since they are not gutted before smoking and retain their full fat content. Most kippers, haddocks and cods are now smoked on a large commercial scale and do not have the same distinctive flavour as fish that has been smoked over oak or apple wood.

*Creamed buckling

Serves 4–6
1 large buckling
1 small onion, finely chopped
grated rind ½ lemon
4 tbsp double cream
seasoning
2 hard-boiled eggs, finely chopped
small pumpernickel rounds
lemon segments

Remove the skin from the buckling. Flake the fish, discarding all the bones. Mix with the onion, lemon rind, cream and seasoning and beat until smooth. Stir in the hard boiled egg. Either put into small cocotte dishes or into one larger dish. Chill for at least 2 hours. Serve with pumpernickel and segments of lemon.

*Taramasalata

Serves 4–6
This is a delicious pale pink fish pâte, with the characteristic tang of smoked cod's roe. It can either be made by hand or blended in a liquidizer. Recipes vary greatly, but this is the one that I prefer.

6 oz smoked cod's roe
2 crushed cloves garlic
juice and grated rind 1 lemon
seasoning
8 tbsp olive oil
6 tbsp double cream

Pound the cod's roe with the crushed garlic, lemon rind and juice, and seasoning. Gradually work in the oil, as for mayonnaise, until the mixture is smooth and creamy. Stir in the cream. A little cochineal may be added to give a deeper pink colour. Chill the taramasalata for at least 1 hour. Serve with fingers of hot toast and black olives.

(American: ⅔ cup smoked cod's roe)

*Smoked potato cakes

Serves 4
1 lb potatoes
seasoning
1½ oz butter
3 tbsp cream
6 oz smoked cod's roe
butter or oil for frying
mayonnaise (see p 60)

Peel the potatoes. Cut into pieces and cook in boiling salted water until just tender. Drain well. Mash the potato with extra seasoning, butter, cream and smoked cod's roe. Divide into 4 portions and form into flat cakes with floured hands. Chill for 1 hour. Heat sufficient butter or oil in a frying pan to give a depth of ¼ in. Add the cakes and fry gently for about 5 minutes on each side. Serve hot with mayonnaise as a snack or as an accompaniment to cooked fish dishes.

Freeze uncooked.

(American: 2 cups mashed potato, 3 tbsp butter, ⅔ cup smoked cod's roe)

Smoked eel cocottes

Serves 4
6 oz smoked eel fillets (see recipe)
⅓ pint cream
seasoning
4 eggs
1½ oz butter

Smoked eel fillets can be bought in vacuum packs from most speciality food shops or delicatessens.

Chop the smoked eel fillets. Mix with half the cream and the seasoning. Spoon into 4 greased cocotte dishes. Carefully crack an egg into each dish. Top with a knob of butter and spoon over the remaining cream. Stand the dishes in a roasting tin, and add sufficient water to come halfway up the sides of the dishes. Cook at 375°F, Mark 5, for about 6–8 minutes so that the whites are set and the yolks still soft. If you prefer a firmer egg, increase the cooking time slightly.

(American: 4–6 slices smoked eel fillets, ¾ cup cream, 3 tbsp butter)

*Brandade

Serves 6–8
This is easily one of the most delicious ways of eating smoked haddock and it makes a little go a long way (smoked cod may be substituted).

1½ lb smoked haddock
milk
½ pint olive oil
¼ pint cream
2 crushed cloves garlic
seasoning
lemon juice
grated nutmeg
triangles of fried bread

Poach the smoked haddock gently in milk until just tender. Drain well. Remove the skin and any bones and flake the fish finely into the top of a double saucepan. Warm the oil and garlic through in one small pan, and the cream in another. Pour a little oil onto the fish and beat with a wooden spoon over the heat. Then add a little cream and beat in. Repeat in this way until you have used up all the oil and cream. Take care not to overheat the brandade, for this may cause it to separate. Season and flavour according to taste with salt, pepper, lemon juice and nutmeg. Spoon the brandade on to a warm serving dish and tuck bread triangles into the edges as a garnish.

(American: 2¼ cups flaked smoked haddock, 1 cup olive oil, ½ cup cream)

Noodles with smoked haddock

Serves 4
1 lb smoked haddock
½ pint milk
½ pint water
seasoning
bay leaf
1½ oz butter
1½ oz flour
3 oz grated cheese
½ lb noodles
3 tbsp toasted breadcrumbs

Poach the smoked haddock for about 10 minutes in the milk and water with seasoning and bay leaf, until just tender. Drain the fish. Remove the skin and any bones and flake the flesh. Melt the butter, add the flour and cook for 1 minute. Gradually add ½ pint of the fish cooking liquid. Bring to the boil and simmer for a few minutes until thickened. Stir in 2 oz of the grated cheese. Cook the noodles in boiling salted water for 10 minutes. Drain thoroughly. Spoon the noodles into a greased ovenproof dish. Top with the flaked fish and spoon over the cheese sauce. Sprinkle with the toasted crumbs and the remaining cheese. Bake at 400°F, Mark 6, for about 20 minutes, until golden brown.

(American: 1½ cups flaked smoked haddock, 1 cup milk, 1 cup water, 3 tbsp butter, 3 tbsp flour, ⅓ cup grated cheese, 1 cup noodles)

*Smoked haddock scallops

Serves 4
These pastry scallops make an unusual and most attractive starter for a dinner party; and they are also very easy to pack for a picnic.

¾ lb shortcrust pastry
1 oz margarine
4 oz mushrooms, sliced
¼ pint milk
¾ lb smoked haddock
3 oz Philadelphia cream cheese
¾ oz cornflour
beaten egg
seasoning

Divide the pastry in half. Roll half the pastry large enough to cut round 4 large saucers. Grease 4 rounded scallop shells. Press a circle of pastry into each shell, leaving a small overlap. Run a finger up and down the natural grooves of the shells. Melt the margarine in a pan and fry the mushrooms gently for 3 minutes. Add the milk and the smoked haddock and simmer gently for 10 minutes. Soften the cream cheese and beat together with the cornflour. Strain the fish and mushrooms. Gradually add the fish liquor to the cream cheese mixture, beating thoroughly to avoid lumps. Flake the fish and mix with the sauce and the mushrooms. Heat gently, stirring until lightly thickened. Season to taste. Allow to cool. Divide the fish mixture amongst the lined scallop shells, leaving a $\frac{1}{2}$ in border of pastry. Roll out the remaining pastry to form lids. Brush the pastry borders with beaten egg. Place the pastry lids over the top and pinch edges to seal. Trim off any excess pastry. Make a small slit in the pastry to allow the steam to escape. Place the shells on a baking sheet. Bake at 400°F, Mark 6, for 25 minutes. Carefully turn the pastry scallops out of their shells and put them back on the baking sheet moulded sides uppermost. Glaze with beaten egg and bake for a further 10–15 minutes. Serve either hot or cold with tartare sauce (see p 61).

(American: 1$\frac{1}{2}$ cups pastry, 2 tbsp margarine, $\frac{2}{3}$ cup mushrooms, $\frac{1}{2}$ cup milk, 1$\frac{1}{4}$ cups flaked smoked haddock, $\frac{1}{2}$ cup cream cheese, 1 tbsp cornflour)

*Chilled smoked haddock soup

Serves 4
$\frac{3}{4}$ pint milk
1 small onion, grated
$\frac{1}{2}$ lb smoked haddock
seasoning
$\frac{1}{4}$ pint soured cream
2 tbsp chopped parsley
4 slices lemon
2 tbsp black lumpfish roe

Put the milk, onion and smoked haddock into a pan. Bring to the boil and simmer for 10 minutes, until the fish is just tender. Remove the fish. Discard any bones and dark skin and flake the fish. Mix the cooking liquor with the flaked smoked haddock, seasoning, soured cream and chopped parsley. Chill for at least 1 hour. Ladle into four small bowls and top with lemon slices and lumpfish roe.

Serve with fried crumbs: heat 2 oz butter in a frying pan. Add 4 tbsp brown breadcrumbs and fry until crisp and golden. Drain before serving.

(American: 1$\frac{1}{2}$ cups milk, $\frac{2}{3}$ cup flaked smoked haddock, $\frac{1}{2}$ cup soured cream, $\frac{1}{4}$ cup butter)

Danish pizza

Serves 4
4 rashers streaky bacon
3 oz melted butter
1 onion, chopped
1 teasp chopped mixed herbs
8 oz can tomatoes, drained
seasoning
6 oz kipper fillets, cut into strips
1 tbsp oil
3 oz Danish Mozzarella cheese, cut into thin slices
6 oz self-raising flour

Grill the bacon rashers until they start to crinkle. Keep to one side. Heat 1 oz of the melted butter and fry the onion gently for 5 minutes. Add the herbs, tomatoes and seasoning and simmer for a further 5 minutes. Add the kipper fillets. Sieve the flour with a good pinch of salt. Add 1 oz of the melted butter and sufficient water to mix to a soft dough. Roll out to a circle about 8½in in diameter. Heat the remaining butter in a large frying pan with the oil. Place the circle of dough in the pan and cook over a moderate heat for 4 minutes to brown the underside. Flip the dough over. Top with the tomato mixture, the bacon rashers and the cheese. Put under a hot grill for about 4 minutes to melt the cheese. Cut into wedges and serve with a salad.

(American: 6 tbsp melted butter, 1 cup canned tomatoes, ⅔ cup kipper fillets, 5 thin slices Danish Mozzarella cheese, ¾ cup self-raising flour)

*Fish lasagne

Serves 6
1 oz butter
1 onion, chopped
1 crushed clove garlic
14 oz can tomatoes
2 tbsp tomato puree
1 teasp caster sugar
1 teasp mixed herbs
seasoning
8 oz kipper fillets, chopped
9 sheets lasagne
½ pint white sauce (see p 60)
3 oz grated cheese

Heat the butter. Fry the onion and garlic gently for 5 minutes. Add the canned tomatoes, tomato puree, sugar, herbs and seasoning. Simmer for 10 minutes. Stir in the chopped kipper. Layer the raw pasta and fish filling in a greased ovenproof dish, finishing with a layer of pasta. Mix the sauce with 2 oz of the grated cheese and spoon over the lasagne. Sprinkle with the remaining cheese. Bake at 375°F, Mark 5, for 25–30 minutes, until bubbling and golden.

(American: 2 tbsp butter, 1½ cups canned tomatoes, 1 cup chopped kipper, approximately 10 sheets lasagne, 1 cup white sauce, ⅓ cup grated cheese)

Kipper and cheese souffle

Serves 4
6 oz kipper fillets, chopped
2 hard-boiled eggs, chopped
3 tbsp cream
seasoning
1 oz butter
1 oz flour
½ pint milk
3 eggs
2 oz grated cheese

Grease 4 individual souffle or deep ovenproof dishes. Mix the chopped kipper with the hard-boiled egg, cream and seasoning. Divide amongst the prepared dishes. Melt the butter in a pan. Stir in the flour and cook for 1 minute. Gradually add the milk and stir over the heat to thicken. Remove from the heat. Beat in the egg yolks and stir over the heat for 1 minute. Remove pan from the heat and beat in the cheese. Cool slightly. Whisk the egg whites until they stand in peaks. Fold gently into the cheese sauce. Spoon the souffle mixture into the dishes. Bake at 425°F, Mark 7, for 6–8 minutes, until well risen and golden. Serve immediately.

(American: $\frac{3}{4}$ cup chopped kipper, 2 tbsp butter, 2 tbsp flour, 1 cup milk, $\frac{1}{4}$ cup grated cheese)

Mackerel and apple cocktails

Serves 4

The combination of crisp apple and smoked mackerel makes a delightful appetizer. Sweet Cox's Orange Pippins are the best apples to use.

1 large smoked mackerel
$\frac{1}{4}$ pint French dressing
$\frac{1}{4}$ pint soured cream
grated rind 1 orange
1 teasp French mustard
seasoning

3 Cox's Orange Pippin apples
watercress

Split the smoked mackerel and remove all the bones. Flake the flesh, discarding the skin if it is tough. Mix the French dressing with the soured cream, orange rind, mustard and seasoning. Core the apples. Chop $2\frac{1}{2}$ of the apples and slice the remaining $\frac{1}{2}$ apple. Mix the chopped apple with the flaked smoked mackerel and divide amongst 4 large scallop shells. Spoon the soured cream dressing over the top. Decorate with the apple slices and sprigs of watercress.

(American: $\frac{1}{2}$ cup French dressing, $\frac{1}{2}$ cup soured cream)

*Smoked salmon koulabiaka

Serves 6

$7\frac{1}{2}$ oz packet frozen puff pastry
3 oz Philadelphia cream cheese
grated rind $\frac{1}{2}$ lemon
cayenne pepper
6 oz sliced smoked salmon
beaten egg

Roll out the puff pastry thinly to a large oblong, approximately 14in by 10in. Soften the cream cheese and mix with the lemon rind. Season with cayenne. Spread evenly over the pastry leaving a $\frac{1}{2}$in space on each of the shorter sides. Lay the smoked salmon over the top. Brush the edges of the short sides with beaten egg. Starting at one of the short sides, carefully roll the pastry and filling together as for a swiss roll. Place on a greased baking sheet. Brush with beaten egg and make several slits in the top surface of the pastry. Bake at 400°F, Mark 6, for $\frac{1}{2}$ hour. Serve warm, cut into slices.

(American: approximately 1 cup puff pastry, $\frac{1}{2}$ cup cream cheese, approximately 8 thin slices smoked salmon)

Smoked trout and lettuce pate

Serves 4–6
1 large smoked trout
grated rind and juice $\frac{1}{2}$ lemon
4 oz unsalted butter, softened
4 tbsp double cream
salt and pepper
6 heart lettuce leaves, finely
   shredded

Remove the skin from the trout. Flake the flesh, discarding all the bones. Mix with the lemon rind and juice, softened butter, cream and seasoning. Beat until smooth. Mix in the shredded lettuce. Spoon into a shallow dish and chill. To serve, the pate can be spooned into hollowed-out lemons, and each lemon stood in a stemmed glass, with crushed ice in the bowl. Accompany with fingers of hot toast.

(American: $\frac{1}{2}$ cup butter)

Gooseberried trout

Serves 4
$\frac{1}{2}$ lb gooseberries
juice of 1 lemon
2–3 oz caster sugar
2 oz butter
4 smoked trout
2 lemons, thinly sliced
3 tbsp chopped parsley

Wash the gooseberries and remove the stems. Put into a pan with the lemon juice and 1 oz of the sugar. Simmer gently for 15 minutes. Push through a sieve to give a smooth puree. Sweeten according to taste and beat in the butter. Chill the sauce. Arrange the smoked trout on a serving dish. Decorate with lemon slices and arrange a ribbon of chopped parsley down the centre of each fish. Serve with the gooseberry sauce and brown bread and butter.

(American: 1 cup gooseberries, 4–6 tbsp caster sugar, $\frac{1}{4}$ cup butter)

Shellfish

This group includes fish varying widely in appearance, shape and flavour. There are two main types: the crustaceans, which have jointed shells, such as crab, crawfish, lobster, prawns and shrimps; and the molluscs, with hinged shells, such as cockles, mussels, oysters, scallops, whelks and winkles. Fresh shellfish are as satisfying and nourishing as best rump steak, being as rich in protein and less fatty. Most simply require boiling, and many can in fact now be bought ready-cooked which saves the bother of cooking them at home. Take special care when buying and cooking them (see pp 5-6 for further details), and bear in mind that some people are allergic to shellfish when planning to serve them to a group.

The following shellfish are available all year round: cockles, prawns, scampi, shrimps, whelks and winkles. From September to March mussels, oysters and scallops can be bought; and from March to October crab, crawfish and lobster.

*Seafood a Gomes de Sa

Serves 6
1½ lb potatoes
⅓ pint oil
2 onions, sliced
1 crushed clove garlic
6 oz peeled prawns
½ lb white crabmeat
3 hard-boiled eggs, sliced
3 oz black olives
chopped parsley
seasoning

Cook the potatoes in boiling salted water for about 10 minutes, until they are just tender but not disintegrating. Remove the skins and cut the potatoes into ¼ in thick slices. Heat 4 tbsp of the oil in a pan. Add the onion and garlic and fry gently for 5 minutes. Put half the potatoes into a well greased oven-proof dish. Top with the shelled prawns and the crab. Season to taste. Add half the fried onions and then the remaining sliced potato. Top with the remaining fried onion and spoon over the rest of the oil. Bake at 375°F, Mark 5, for ½ hour. Garnish with sliced egg, olives and chopped parsley.

Freeze without garnish.

(American: approximately 4 cups sliced potato, ⅔ cup oil, ¾ cup crabmeat, 1 cup peeled prawns, ⅓ cup black olives)

Seafood spaghetti

Serves 4
8 oz spaghetti
6 rashers bacon, chopped
1 oz butter
1 onion, chopped
1 crushed clove garlic
4 oz mushrooms, sliced
6 oz Philadelphia cream cheese
¼ pint milk
seasoning
4 oz peeled prawns
grated Parmesan cheese

Cook spaghetti in boiling salted water for 10 minutes. Drain thoroughly. Fry the bacon in the butter for 5–6 minutes. Add the chopped onion and the crushed garlic and fry gently for 5 minutes. Add the sliced mushrooms and fry for a further 2 minutes. Blend the cream cheese with the milk, beating to avoid any lumps. Add the cream cheese mixture to the vegetables and bacon, and bring to the boil. Add the cooked spaghetti and prawns and stir over a gentle heat until heated through. Pile into a serving dish and sprinkle with Parmesan cheese before serving.

(American: 4 servings of spaghetti, 2 tbsp butter, 1 cup sliced mushrooms, 1 cup cream cheese, ½ cup milk, ⅔ cup peeled prawns)

*Indian-style shellfish

Serves 4

This is a great dish for curry lovers. It is hot and spicy, but not too hot to mask the flavour of the fish.

1 pint prawns in their shells
½ pint dry white wine
2 pints mussels
1 onion, chopped
1 crushed clove garlic
2 oz butter
3 teasp curry powder
1 oz flour
¼ pint light chicken stock
½ pint cream
juice ½ lemon
seasoning
plain boiled rice

Remove the shells from the prawns and put into a pan with the white wine. Simmer for 10 minutes, and drain off the fish liquor. Steam the mussels in a colander over boiling water until the shells open. Remove the mussels from the their shells. Fry the onion and garlic gently in the butter for 5 minutes. Stir in the curry powder and cook for 1 minute. Add the flour and cook for a further minute. Gradually add the fish liquid and the stock and simmer for 10 minutes. Add the cream, lemon juice, seasoning, prawns and mussels and bring just to the boil. Simmer 1 minute. Serve with plain boiled rice.

(American: 2 cups prawns in their shells, 1 cup white wine, 4 cups mussels, ¼ cup butter, 2 tbsp flour, ½ cup stock, 1 cup cream)

Zarzuela

Serves 6

Apart from paella, *this is probably one of the most renowned of Spanish fish dishes. This recipe is for a simple version.*

1½ lb cooked lobster (see Lobster Gourmet, p 48)
12 large prawns in their shells
3 tbsp olive oil
1 onion, chopped
2 crushed cloves garlic
1 green pepper, finely chopped
14 oz can tomatoes, drained
2 oz ground almonds
good pinch powdered saffron
seasoning
¾ pint white wine
½ pint water
3 tbsp brandy
squeeze of lemon juice
12 fresh mussels, scrubbed and cleaned
2 oz shelled cockles
½ lb shelled scallops, cut into pieces
chopped parsley

Remove the flesh from the cooked lobster and cut into pieces. Remove the heads and any eggs from the prawns, leaving the tail shell on. Heat the olive oil and fry the onion,

garlic and pepper for 5 minutes.
Add the drained tomatoes, ground
almonds, saffron and seasoning.
Bring to the boil and cook briskly
for about 5–6 minutes, until the
mixture is quite thick. Add the wine,
water, brandy and lemon juice and
bring back to the boil. Add the
mussels, cover the pan and cook for
10 minutes. Add the lobster,
prawns, cockles and scallops and
simmer for a further 5 minutes.
(Discard any mussels that have not
opened.) Serve the zarzuela straight
from the pan, sprinkled with
chopped parsley.

(American: medium size lobster, 1
cup canned tomatoes, 4 tbsp
ground almonds, $1\frac{1}{2}$ cups white
wine, 1 cup water, $\frac{1}{3}$ cup shelled
cockles, approximately 8 shelled
scallops)

Fisherman's stroganoff

Serves 4
2 oz butter
1 onion, chopped
1 crushed clove garlic
4 oz button mushrooms, sliced
1 oz flour
$\frac{1}{2}$ pint white wine
$\frac{1}{4}$ pint soured cream
seasoning
4 oz shelled prawns
4 oz shelled, cooked mussels (see
recipe)

grated rind $\frac{1}{2}$ lemon
chopped parsley

Most fishmongers sell shelled
cooked mussels by weight, which
saves you having to cook them.

Heat the butter in a pan and fry the
onion and garlic gently for 5
minutes. Add the sliced mushrooms
and cook for 2 minutes. Stir in the
flour and cook for 1 minute.
Gradually add the white wine. Bring
to the boil and simmer until
thickened. Stir in the soured cream,
seasoning, prawns and mussels.
Heat through for 3 minutes. Spoon
into a serving dish and sprinkle with
lemon rind and chopped parsley.
Serve with cooked pasta or rice.

(American: $\frac{1}{4}$ cup butter, 1 cup sliced
mushrooms, 2 tbsp flour, 1 cup
white wine, $\frac{1}{2}$ cup soured cream,
$\frac{2}{3}$ cup peeled prawns, $\frac{2}{3}$ cup shelled
mussels)

Surprise pan bagna

Serves 4
1 large French loaf
seasoning
1 can anchovy fillets
5 tbsp olive oil
2 oz smoked salmon butter (see p 62)
4 oz shelled shrimps or prawns
2 oz shelled cockles
4 tbsp mayonnaise (see p 60)

Cut the French loaf in half lengthways. Sprinkle each half with 2 tbsp

lightly salted water. Drain the anchovy fillets and mix the oil from the can with the olive oil. Spoon evenly over the crumb side of each half of the loaf. Leave for $\frac{1}{2}$ hour. Spread the bread lightly with smoked salmon butter. Top one half of the loaf with the shelled shrimps or prawns, cockles, chopped anchovy fillets and mayonnaise. Season. Sandwich together with the other half loaf. Wrap in a damp tea towel. Put a fairly heavy weight over the top and leave for $\frac{1}{2}$ hour. Unwrap the loaf and cut into thick slices.

(American: $\frac{1}{4}$ cup smoked salmon butter, $\frac{2}{3}$ cup peeled prawns or shrimps, $\frac{1}{3}$ cup cockles)

Dressed crab

Serves 4

I include this basic recipe to show how to deal with a whole crab. There are several parts of the crab which must be removed and discarded.

2 medium size crabs
French dressing (see p 61)
seasoning
1 hard-boiled egg
chopped parsley
paprika
chantilly sauce (see p 61)

It is more convenient to buy crabs that have been cooked by the fish-monger but if you prefer to buy them live, drop them into a pan of seasoned water, onion and herbs and boil until they rise to the top of the pan.

Twist off the claws, keeping the smaller ones for decoration. Crack the large claws with nut-crackers and scoop the meat into a basin, discarding any tendons. Turn the crab onto its back shell, and prise up the apron (flap). Add the white meat from the shell to the claw meat. Remove the small sac and the pointed gills ('dead men's fingers'), and any green matter. Throw all three away. Put the dark meat into a separate basin and scrape out any extra white meat. Tap the inside edge of the shells and break along their natural markings. Wipe the insides with a damp cloth. Season both dark and white meats. Moisten the white meat with French dressing and add the chopped white from the hard-boiled egg (keep the yolk for garnish). Many people mix the dark meat with breadcrumbs to thicken it, but this gives a rather cloying flavour and spoils the crab— it is better to chill it. Spoon the white meat into either side of each shell, leaving a space down the centre. Fill the space with the dark meat. Decorate the dark meat with alternate bands of chopped parsley, sieved hard boiled egg yolk and paprika. Decorate the dish with the small claws and serve with chantilly sauce.

Creole crab gumbo

Serves 4
1½ oz butter
1 onion, chopped
1 crushed clove garlic
1 green pepper, seeded and chopped
14 oz can tomatoes
¼ pint single cream
2 egg yolks
¾ lb crabmeat
seasoning

Heat the butter in a pan. Add the onion and garlic and fry together for 5 minutes. Add the chopped pepper, and fry for a further 3 minutes. Add the canned tomatoes and simmer for 20 minutes. Blend the cream with the egg yolks, and add a little of the hot vegetable liquid. Add to the ingredients in the pan and stir over a gentle heat until lightly thickened. Add the crabmeat, season to taste and heat through gently. Serve very hot, with chunks of crusty bread.

(American: 3 tbsp butter, 1½ cups canned tomatoes, ½ cup cream, 1¼ cups crabmeat)

*Crab vols au vent

Serves 6
6 baked vol au vent cases, 3½in in diameter

½ pint egg sauce (see p 60)
½ lb crabmeat
seasoning
parsley
avocado mayonnaise (see p 61)

Heat the vol au vent cases through in a moderate oven. Mix the egg sauce with the crabmeat and season to taste. Divide between the vol au vent cases. Return to the oven for 10 minutes to warm the filling through. Serve hot garnished with sprigs of parsley, and accompanied by avocado mayonnaise.

(American: 1 cup egg sauce, ¾ cup crabmeat)

Lobster gourmet

Serves 4
2 lobsters, about 1½ lb each
½ pint mornay sauce (see p 60)
3 tbsp double cream, whipped
3 oz peeled prawns
1 tbsp brandy
seasoning
3 oz smoked salmon butter (see p 62)

It is more convenient to buy the lobsters from your fishmonger ready prepared—cooked and split in half. If, however, you prefer to prepare the lobsters yourself: make sure that the pincers are tied together, to prevent being pinched. Plunge the lobsters into a pan of boiling water and cook for approximately 20 minutes. Remove them from the pan and lay on a board, back shell uppermost. Using a sharp pointed knife, split them through lengthwise. Remove the stomach from the head end of the lobster and the black intestinal line from the tail end.

Remove as much of the lobster flesh as possible without puncturing the underneath shell. Cut the flesh into pieces. Crack the claws. Remove the flesh, cut it into pieces and add to the rest of the lobster flesh. Mix the lobster flesh with the mornay sauce, cream, prawns, brandy and seasoning. Spoon back into the half lobster shells. Bake at 400°F, Mark 6, for 15 minutes. Top with knobs of smoked salmon butter before serving.

(American: 2 medium size lobsters, 1 cup mornay sauce, ½ cup peeled prawns, 6 tbsp smoked salmon butter)

Six minute moules marinieres

Serves 4
1 onion, grated
⅓ pint white wine
⅓ pint bottled Italian garlic dressing
2 oz butter
seasoning
4 pints mussels, scrubbed
chopped parsley

Put the grated onion, white wine, Italian garlic dressing, butter and seasoning into a large pan. Bring to the boil. Add the mussels, cover the pan, and cook for 5 minutes. Spoon into soup bowls and sprinkle with chopped parsley. Serve with plenty of crusty bread.

(American: 8 generous cups mussels, ⅔ cup white wine, ⅔ cup Italian garlic dressing, ¼ cup butter)

Oysters au gratin

Serves 6
4 dozen oysters
½ lb herb butter (see p 62)
seasoning
3 oz finely grated cheese
4 tbsp breadcrumbs

Open the oysters carefully, using the special tool for the purpose. Drain off and reserve the excess liquid to drink or use in a soup or sauce. Place the oysters in their deep shells. Stand on oyster plates and top each oyster with a small knob of herb butter. Season. Mix the grated cheese and the breadcrumbs and sprinkle over the oysters. Cook at 375°F, Mark 5, for 10 minutes.

(American: 1 cup herb butter, ⅓ cup grated cheese)

*Watercress and oyster soup

Serves 4
This is an excellent way of making a few oysters go a long way.

3 bunches watercress
1¼ pints stock
seasoning
grated rind ½ lemon
3 oz Philadelphia cream cheese
8 oysters
thin lemon slices

Remove the thick stalks from the watercress. Wash the leaf parts and chop coarsely. Put the chopped watercress into a pan with the stock, seasoning and lemon rind. Bring to the boil and simmer gently for 15 minutes. Either sieve the soup or blend in a liquidizer. Return the soup to the pan. Blend the cream cheese with a little of the soup and beat until smooth. Add to the remaining soup. Open the oysters, adding their liquid to the pan. Release the oysters from their shells and add to the soup. Heat through for 3 minutes. Serve in small bowls, garnished with sliced lemon.

(American: 2½ cups stock, ½ cup cream cheese)

*Coquilles St Jacques estragon

Serves 4
8 scallops
¼ pint white wine
1 small onion, quartered
1 bay leaf
seasoning
1 tbsp chopped fresh tarragon
1 oz butter
1 oz flour
¼ pint milk
4 tbsp cream
grated rind ½ lemon
2 oz grated cheese
mashed potato
parsley

Remove the scallops from their shells. Discard the beards. Slice the white part of the scallops. Put into a pan with the red scallop tails, the wine, onion, bay leaf, seasoning and tarragon. Cover the pan and poach gently for 8 minutes. Melt the butter in a pan. Add the flour and cook for 1 minute. Gradually add the milk and the fish cooking liquor (without the bay leaf and onion). Bring to the boil and stir over a gentle heat until thickened. Remove from the heat and beat in the cream, lemon rind, grated cheese and seasoning. Pipe mashed potato around the edge of 4 scallop shells. Spoon a little sauce into each shell and then top with the cooked scallop. Spoon over the remaining sauce. Bake at 425°F, Mark 7, for 12–15 minutes. Garnish with parsley before serving.

(American: ½ cup white wine, 2 tbsp butter, 2 tbsp flour, ½ cup milk, ¼ cup grated cheese)

Scampi alla marinara

Serves 4
20 large scampi in their shells
⅔ pint white wine
4 tbsp olive oil
4 tbsp chopped parsley
1 small onion, finely chopped
1 crushed clove garlic
2 tbsp fresh white breadcrumbs
5 tomatoes, peeled, seeded and
    finely chopped
1 hard-boiled egg
seasoning

Rinse the scampi and dry. Put into
a shallow dish with 3 tbsp of the
white wine, 2 tbsp of the olive oil
and half the parsley. Cover the dish
and leave in the refrigerator for 3
hours. Heat the remaining 2 tbsp
oil. Add the onion and garlic and
cook gently for 5 minutes. Stir in the
breadcrumbs, tomato and the
sieved hard-boiled egg yolk (the
white is used for garnish). Simmer
for about 5 minutes, until the
mixture becomes a thick puree. Put
the scampi into a pan with its
marinade and the remaining wine
and oil. Season to taste. Simmer
gently for 10 minutes. Add the
tomato and onion mixture and heat
through for 2–3 minutes. Put into a
serving dish. Sprinkle with the
chopped hard-boiled egg white and
garnish with small wedges of lemon.
The only way to eat this delicious
scampi dish is with fingers. Serve
plenty of chunky bread to mop up
the juices and small bowls of water
for rinsing the fingers.

(American: 1¼ cups wine)

Scampi newburg

Serves 4
2 oz butter
1 small onion, finely chopped
1 crushed clove garlic
24 scampi, shelled
1 tbsp tomato puree
seasoning
½ pint cream
2 egg yolks
3 tbsp brandy
plain boiled rice

Heat the butter and fry the onion
and garlic gently for 5 minutes. Add
the shelled scampi and stir over the
heat for 2 minutes. Stir in the
tomato puree and seasoning. Mix
the cream with the egg yolks and
brandy. Add to the scampi and heat
through gently; do not allow the
sauce to boil vigorously. Serve the
scampi newburg on a bed of cooked
rice.

(American: ¼ cup butter, 1 cup
cream)

Preserved fish

This group covers frozen, canned and bottled fish. Since they are not highly perishable preserved fish can usefully be kept in the freezer or store cupboard and eaten at any time of the year, so they are good standbys. As with all frozen food, frozen fish has a fixed shelf-life which varies according to the type of fish (see pp 5-6). Fish bought ready-frozen is date stamped. Most bottled fish is best stored in the refrigerator even when it is unopened.

Canned and bottled fish are ready to eat with or without heating. They are all packaged in strictly hygienic conditions and top quality fish is used, so they are unlikely to cause stomach upsets. They are preserved by being cooked in their containers at a very high temperature with all the air excluded. Avoid buying any 'bulging' cans or jars with domed lids. This is a sign that the can or jar has 'blown', and that a harmful gas has formed inside.

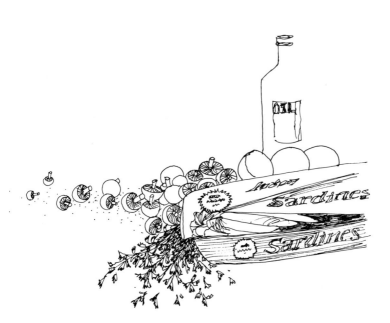

Anchoyade

Serves 4
1 can anchovy fillets
2 crushed cloves garlic
3 tbsp olive oil
juice ½ lemon
ground black pepper
4 thick slices French bread
fine breadcrumbs
chopped parsley

Tip the anchovy fillets and their oil into a basin. Pound with a wooden spoon until smooth. Add the crushed garlic, olive oil, lemon juice, and black pepper to taste. Spread generously over the slices of French bread. Sprinkle with fine bread-crumbs and chopped parsley. Put onto a baking sheet and bake at 375°F, Mark 5, for about 15–20 minutes. Serve as a snack or starter.

(American: ¼ cup anchovy fillets)

*Clam chowder

Serves 4
1 oz butter
1 tbsp oil
1 onion, finely chopped
1½ oz flour
¾ pint chicken stock
1 small can clams
8 oz can sweetcorn kernels
salt and pepper
¼ pint soured cream
2 tbsp chopped parsley

Heat the butter and oil. Fry the chopped onion gently for 5 minutes. Stir in the flour and cook for 1 minute. Gradually add the chicken stock and bring to the boil, stirring. Add the clams, including their liquid, the sweetcorn and seasoning. Simmer for 20 minutes. Add the soured cream and chopped parsley and heat through gently. Serve with small triangles of toast.

(American: 2 tbsp butter, 3 tbsp flour, 1½ cups chicken stock, ½ cup clams, ⅔ cup sweetcorn kernels, ½ cup soured cream)

*Danablu cod's roe pate

Serves 4–6
7½ oz can cod's roe
4 oz Danablu cheese, crumbled
2 oz butter
2 tbsp cream
seasoning
3 oz finely chopped walnuts
black grapes

Crumble the cod's roe in a bowl with a fork. Add the crumbled Danablu cheese, butter and cream and work together until smooth. Season to taste and add the chopped walnuts. Oil a sheet of greaseproof paper. Put the pate onto the oiled paper and form into a sausage shape. Roll up in the paper, twisting each end like a Christmas cracker to secure the pate. Serve cut in slices, garnished with black grapes and accompanied by fingers of hot toast.

(American: approx $\frac{3}{4}$ cup canned cod's roe, $\frac{1}{2}$ cup crumbled Danablu cheese, $\frac{1}{4}$ cup butter, $\frac{1}{3}$ cup walnuts)

Aalborg Akvavit herring

Serves 4
4 rollmop herrings
$\frac{1}{3}$ pint vinegar
3 tbsp caster sugar
2 bay leaves
10 crushed peppercorns
1$\frac{1}{2}$ teasp dill seed
1 small onion, sliced
$\frac{1}{8}$ pint Aalborg Akvavit

Soak the rollmop herrings in water for 24 hours. Drain thoroughly. Mix the vinegar, sugar, crushed peppercorns, bay leaves and dill seed. Put the herrings into a shallow dish. Add the vinegar mixture, sliced onion and Akvavit. Cover the dish and refrigerate for 12 hours. Serve with coarse rye bread, a bowl of soured cream, and a glass of Akvavit for each person.

(American: $\frac{3}{4}$ cup vinegar, $\frac{1}{4}$ cup Akvavit)

Master mariner danwich

Serves 4
4 thin slices pumpernickel or rye
    bread
butter
4 canned Matjes herring fillets
2 tomatoes, sliced
1 small onion, cut into rings
seasoning
4 tbsp soured cream

Spread the pumpernickel generously with butter right to the edges. Drain the herrings. Cut each one into three or four pieces and arrange on top of the buttered bread. Top with sliced tomato and onion rings and season to taste. Spoon soured cream on top.

*New-style macaroni cheese

Serves 6
6 oz short cut macaroni
3 rashers streaky bacon, chopped
1 onion, finely chopped
1 oz butter
1 pint white sauce (see p 60)
salt and pepper
1 teasp made mustard
8 oz can kipper fillets
4 oz grated cheese

Cook the macaroni in boiling salted water for 8 minutes. Drain thoroughly. Fry the bacon and onion gently in the butter for 5 minutes. Stir in the sauce, seasoning and mustard. Drain the kipper fillets and chop. Add the chopped kipper, half the cheese and the drained macaroni to the sauce, and mix together. Spoon into a greased ovenproof dish and sprinkle with the remaining grated cheese. Bake at 375°F, Mark 5, for 25 minutes.

(American: 1 cup short cut macaroni, 2 tbsp butter, 2 cups white sauce, ⅔ cup canned kipper fillets, ½ cup grated cheese)

Fish tetrazzini

Serves 4–6
8 oz spaghetti
salt and pepper
3 oz butter
2 oz flour
¾ pint chicken stock
¼ pint cream
2 tbsp sherry
4 oz sliced mushrooms
8 oz jar mussels in brine
small can calamares

Cook the spaghetti in plenty of boiling salted water for 10 minutes, until just tender. Drain well. Melt 2 oz of the butter in a pan. Add the flour and cook for 1 minute. Gradually stir in the chicken stock away from the heat. Return to the heat and stir until lightly thickened. Simmer for 3 minutes. Stir in the cream and sherry and season to taste. Fry the sliced mushrooms in the remaining 1 oz butter for 5 minutes. Put half the sauce into a pan with the spaghetti and heat through gently. Add the mushrooms, drained mussels and calamares to the remaining sauce and heat through. Spoon the spaghetti into a warm serving dish and top with the fish and mushroom sauce.

(American: 6 tbsp butter, ¼ cup flour, 1½ cups chicken stock, ½ cup cream, ⅔ cup mushrooms, approximately 1 cup drained mussels, ⅓ cup canned calamares)

Potato mussel cake

Serves 4
1 onion, thinly sliced
2 rashers bacon, chopped
2 tbsp oil
3 medium size cooked potatoes, chopped
5 eggs
salt and pepper
5 oz jar mussels

Fry the onion and bacon gently in oil, in a large frying pan, for 5 minutes. Add the chopped potato and stir over the heat for 3 minutes. Beat the eggs with salt and pepper and stir in the drained mussels. Pour the egg mixture into the pan, and stir occasionally over the heat as it starts to set. Once the 'cake' or omelette has set on the underside, put it under a hot grill until the top is risen and golden brown. Cut into wedges and serve immediately.

(American: ½ cup mussels)

Provencale pasta salad

Serves 4–6

This is a colourful Mediterranean-style salad and is a good choice as a starter or for a buffet meal. Serve it with crusty bread, and a 'crisp' white wine.

8 oz pasta shells
seasoning
¼ pint French dressing (see p 61)
1 crisp lettuce
3 hard-boiled eggs
¼ pint mayonnaise (see p 60)
6 anchovy fillets
1 large can pilchards in tomato sauce
2 tomatoes
1 green pepper
12 black olives

Cook the pasta shells in boiling salted water for 7–8 minutes, until just tender. Drain the pasta shells thoroughly and toss in the French dressing while still warm. Cover a large oval dish with a bed of washed lettuce. Halve the eggs and place down the centre of the dish. Arrange the cooked pasta in a border around the outside of the dish. Put the pilchards in their sauce between the eggs and the pasta. Spoon a little mayonnaise over each egg and top with a curled anchovy fillet. Spoon the remaining mayonnaise over the pilchards and top with sliced tomato. Sprinkle the pasta shells with finely chopped green pepper and garnish the dish with black olives.

(American: ½ cup French dressing, ½ cup mayonnaise, 1¼ cups canned pilchards)

Noodle and prawn kugel

Serves 4–6

4 oz short cut noodles
salt and pepper
2 oz butter
¼ pint soured cream
8 oz cottage cheese with chives
1 oz grated Parmesan cheese
2 eggs
¼ pint white sauce (see p 60)
¼ pint mayonnaise (see p 60)
1½ tbsp tomato puree
1 teasp caster sugar
few drops Tabasco
6 oz can peeled prawns
3½ oz can smoked oysters

Cook the noodles in plenty of boiling salted water for 8 minutes. Drain thoroughly. Melt the butter in a pan and add the cooked noodles. Blend together the soured cream, cottage cheese and Parmesan cheese and add to the cooked noodles. Season with salt and pepper and bind with the beaten eggs. Oil a 1-pint ring mould and pack in the noodles mixture. Cover with greased paper. Bake at 375°F, Mark 5, for 45 minutes. Meanwhile make the sauce: put the white sauce, mayonnaise, tomato puree, caster sugar and a few drops Tabasco into a pan. Rinse the canned prawns in cold water. Drain and add to the ingredients in the pan. Heat the sauce through. Turn out the cooked noodle mould on a warm serving dish. Spoon the prawn sauce into the centre and garnish with smoked oysters.

(American: $\frac{2}{3}$ cup short cut noodles, $\frac{1}{4}$ cup butter, $\frac{1}{2}$ cup soured cream, 1 cup cottage cheese, 2 tbsp grated Parmesan cheese, $\frac{1}{2}$ cup white sauce, $\frac{1}{2}$ cup mayonnaise, $\frac{1}{2}$ cup canned prawns, $\frac{1}{4}$ cup smoked oysters)

*Salmon and cucumber mousse

Serves 4–6
$7\frac{1}{2}$ oz can red or pink salmon
grated rind and juice $\frac{1}{2}$ lemon
seasoning
pinch cayenne pepper
$\frac{1}{4}$ pint natural yogurt
$\frac{1}{4}$ pint mayonnaise (see p 60)
3 rounded teasp powdered gelatine
$\frac{1}{2}$ small cucumber, seeded and
    chopped
lemon slices
parsley

Mix the salmon with the lemon rind and juice, seasonings, yogurt and mayonnaise. Dissolve the gelatine

in 1 tbsp water over a gentle heat and add to the salmon mixture. Stir in the finely chopped cucumber. When the mousse is on the point of setting, either spoon into one large dish or into small individual dishes. Refrigerate until needed. Decorate with lemon slices and parsley before serving.

(American: approximately $\frac{3}{4}$ cup canned salmon, $\frac{1}{2}$ cup natural yogurt, $\frac{1}{2}$ cup mayonnaise)

*Dolmathes

Serves 4
8 large green cabbage leaves
1 onion, finely chopped
2 tbsp oil
8 tbsp cooked rice
$7\frac{1}{2}$ oz can salmon or tuna, flaked
2 tbsp chopped parsley
$1\frac{1}{2}$ oz chopped nuts
grated rind $\frac{1}{2}$ lemon
beaten egg
salt and pepper
8 oz can tomatoes
2 tbsp dry white wine
2 tbsp olive oil

Remove the coarse centre stem from each cabbage leaf. Plunge the leaves into a pan of boiling salted water and cook for 2 minutes to make them more pliable. Drain on absorbent paper. Fry the chopped onion gently in the oil for 5 minutes. Mix with the cooked rice, flaked fish, parsley, nuts and grated lemon rind. Add sufficient beaten egg to bind, and season to taste. Divide the mixture amongst the cabbage leaves. Mould each leaf around the mixture to completely enclose the filling, and make 8 small 'cabbages'. Arrange them close together in a greased ovenproof dish. Mix the canned tomatoes with the white wine and olive oil and spoon over the dolmathes. Cover with a lid or a piece of greased foil and cook at 375°F, Mark 5, for 45 minutes.

(American: ¾ cup canned fish, 3 tbsp chopped nuts, ¾ cup canned tomatoes)

Stuffed mushrooms

Serves 4
24 small button mushrooms
6 oz can sardines
2 hard-boiled eggs, chopped
seasoning
juice of 1 lemon
4 tbsp oil
3 tbsp chopped parsley

Remove the stalks from the mushrooms and wipe them. Put the mushrooms into a shallow pan and add the drained oil from the sardines, seasoning, lemon juice, oil and parsley. Simmer for 4 minutes. Remove the mushrooms and drain on absorbent paper. Mash the sardines and mix with the chopped hard-boiled egg. Spoon some sardine mixture into each mushroom. Put the mushrooms into a shallow hors d'oeuvre dish and pour over the cooking liquid. Chill for at least 2 hours before serving.

(American: ⅔ cup canned sardines)

*Shrimp and artichoke chevreuse

Serves 4
Brittany Prince artichokes are the best for this recipe.

2 Brittany artichokes
½ lb button mushrooms, coarsely
  chopped
1 onion, chopped
2 oz butter
small can peeled shrimps
1 pint white sauce (see p 60)
1½ teasp French mustard
seasoning
grated Parmesan cheese

Boil the artichokes in the usual way. Cut into quarters and remove the chokes. Gently fry the chopped onion in butter for 4 minutes. Add the chopped mushrooms and continue cooking for a further 4 minutes. Put the quartered artichokes into a greased ovenproof dish and add the fried mushroom, onion and shrimps. Mix the sauce with the French mustard and seasoning and spoon over the artichokes. Sprinkle with grated Parmesan cheese. Bake at 400°F, Mark 6, for 20 minutes, until lightly golden and bubbling. Serve immediately.

(American: approximately 1¼ cups chopped mushrooms, ¼ cup butter, 2 cups white sauce)

*Floating skipper cocktails

Serves 4
2 × 3¾ oz cans John West skippers brisling
2 teasp tomato puree
grated rind ½ lemon
3 tbsp fresh white breadcrumbs
3 tbsp soured cream
seasoning
4 large lemons
4 sprigs parsley

Mash the skippers with the tomato puree, grated lemon rind, bread-crumbs, soured cream and seasoning. Chill for 1 hour. Cut a thin slice from the top of each lemon. Carefully hollow out the lemons, removing as much of the flesh and membrane as possible. Wipe the insides with absorbent paper. Then spoon the skipper filling into the lemons. Put a small sprig of parsley into four narrow, stemmed wine glasses and fill almost to the top with cold water. Carefully sit a lemon in the top of each glass.

Serve with pumpernickel or rye bread.

(American: approximately ¾ cup canned oily fish)

Cauliflower tonnato salad

Serves 4
7½ oz can tuna fish
can anchovy fillets
grated rind and juice ½ lemon
seasoning
3 tbsp capers
¼ pint mayonnaise (see p 60)
1 tbsp white wine vinegar
1 medium size Brittany Prince cauliflower

Put the tuna fish with its oil into a basin. Add the anchovy fillets with their oil, the lemon rind and juice, 2 tbsp capers and the mayonnaise. Mash together until well mixed; for a smoother sauce the ingredients can be blended in a liquidizer. Stir in the wine vinegar, and a little hot water if the sauce is too thick. Divide the cauliflower into florets. Cook in boiling salted water for 10 minutes. Drain well and toss the florets in the tuna sauce while it is still warm. Allow to cool and then chill before serving. Garnish with the remaining capers.

(American: ¾ cup canned tuna, ½ cup mayonnaise)

Sauces to serve with fish

This section gives a number of savoury sauces and butters to serve with fish, as well as a few batter recipes for coating fish to be fried.

Basic white sauce

Makes $\frac{1}{2}$ pint
This is the basis for many sauces served with fish.

1 oz butter or margarine
1 oz flour
$\frac{1}{4}$ pint milk
$\frac{1}{4}$ pint stock (or liquid from cooking fish)
seasoning

Melt the butter in a pan. Stir in the flour and cook for 30 seconds. Gradually add the milk and stock, stirring. Bring to the boil and simmer 2 minutes. Season to taste. This gives a coating consistency.

For a pouring sauce: use 1 pint liquid.

(American: 2 tbsp butter, $\frac{1}{2}$ cup milk, $\frac{1}{2}$ cup stock)

Veloute sauce
Beat 3 tbsp cream and 1 egg yolk into $\frac{1}{2}$ pint basic white sauce.

Chaufroid sauce
Add $\frac{1}{2}$ oz dissolved gelatine to $\frac{1}{2}$ pint basic white sauce. When thickened use to glaze cold cooked fish.

(American: 3 teasp gelatine)

Anchovy sauce
Add 1-2 teasp anchovy essence to $\frac{1}{2}$ pint basic white sauce.

Curry sauce
Add 1–2 teasp curry paste to $\frac{1}{2}$ pint basic white sauce.

Maitre d'hotel sauce
Add juice $\frac{1}{2}$ lemon, 2 tbsp chopped parsley and 2 tbsp cream to $\frac{1}{2}$ pint basic white sauce.

Mornay sauce
Add 3 oz grated cheese to $\frac{1}{2}$ pint basic white sauce. Spoon over cooked fish and brown under the grill or in the oven.

(American: $\frac{1}{3}$ cup cheese)

Mustard sauce
Add 4 teasp made French mustard to $\frac{1}{2}$ pint basic white sauce.

Egg sauce
Add 2 chopped hard-boiled eggs to $\frac{1}{2}$ pint basic white sauce.

Mayonnaise

Makes $\frac{1}{2}$ pint

2 egg yolks
1 tbsp wine vinegar
1 teasp French mustard
$\frac{1}{2}$ pint olive oil

pinch caster sugar
seasoning

Beat the egg yolks with the vinegar. Add the mustard. Gradually add the oil, in a fine trickle, whisking all the time. Once most of the oil has been used, you can add it more quickly. Add the sugar and seasoning. If too thick, add a little vinegar or lemon juice.

(American: 1 cup oil)

Chantilly sauce
Mix $\frac{1}{4}$ pint mayonnaise with $\frac{1}{4}$ pint lightly whipped cream.

(American: $\frac{1}{2}$ cup mayonnaise, $\frac{1}{2}$ cup cream)

Tartare sauce
Add 2 tbsp chopped parsley, 1 tbsp capers and 2 tbsp chopped gherkin to $\frac{1}{2}$ pint mayonnaise.

Maltaise sauce
Add grated rind 1 orange and 1 tbsp marmalade to $\frac{1}{2}$ pint mayonnaise.

Avocado mayonnaise
Mash the flesh of 1 ripe avocado with grated rind $\frac{1}{2}$ lemon and mix with $\frac{1}{2}$ pint mayonnaise.

Hollandaise sauce

Makes $\frac{1}{2}$ pint

2 tbsp vinegar
1 teasp crushed peppercorns
4 tbsp water
3 egg yolks

6 oz melted butter
seasoning
few drops lemon juice

Boil the vinegar, peppercorns and water in a small pan until reduced by one third. Strain into the top of a double saucepan or a basin over a pan of hot water. Whisk in the egg yolks over a gentle heat until mixture begins to thicken. Add the butter in a thin stream, whisking all the time, until smooth and well blended. Season and flavour with lemon juice.

(American: $\frac{3}{4}$ cup butter)

French dressing (or vinaigrette)

French dressing is used in several of the fish recipes in this book, as well as being used to dress salads. The proportions of oil to vinegar vary according to taste, but the following quantities give a very palatable dressing: 6 tbsp olive oil mixed with 2 tbsp white wine vinegar, 1 teasp French mustard and seasoning. Shake in a screw top bottle or jar (makes $\frac{1}{4}$ pint).

Basic batter

A batter is best made $\frac{1}{2}$–1 hour before you need to use it so that it has a chance to relax.

4 oz plain flour
good pinch salt

1 egg
¼ pint milk or ale

Sieve the flour and salt. Add the egg
and a little of the liquid. Beat until
smooth. Gradually beat in the
remaining liquid. Beat hard until
bubbles form.

(American: 1 cup flour, ½ cup liquid)

Egg white batter

*A very light batter, suitable for
prawns and scampi.*

4 oz plain flour
pinch salt
1 tbsp olive oil
¼ pint lukewarm water or beer
white of 1 large egg

Mix the sieved flour and salt with the
oil and gradually beat in the liquid
until smooth. Cover and leave to
stand for 1 hour. Fold in the stiffly
beaten egg white just before using.

(American: 1 cup flour, ½ cup liquid)

Savoury butters

*These make an interesting and tasty
accompaniment to cooked fish.*

Cream 4 oz butter with seasoning
and one of the following
flavourings:
2 teasp grated horseradish
1–2 tbsp chopped fresh herbs
2 oz chopped smoked salmon
    trimmings
1 tbsp French mustard

Roll in a piece of greaseproof paper
and chill. Cut into slices to serve.

(American: ½ cup butter)

Index